MAX LUCADO

LIFE LESSONS *from* 2 SAMUEL

God's Guidance in the Crossroads of Life

Published by HarperChristian Resources, 3950 Sparks Drive SE, Suite 101, Grand Rapids, MI 49546, USA. HarperChristian Resources is a registered trademark of HarperCollins Christian Publishing, Inc.

Requests for information should be addressed to customercare@harpercollins.com.

ISBN 978-0-310-17097-6 (softcover)
ISBN 978-0-310-17098-3 (ebook)

HarperChristian Resources titles may be purchased in bulk for church, business, fundraising, or ministry use. For information, please e-mail ResourceSpecialist@ChurchSource.com.

HarperCollins Publishers, Macken House, 39/40 Mayor Street Upper, Dublin 1, D01 C9W8, Ireland (https://www.harpercollins.com).

CONTENTS

HOW TO STUDY THE BIBLE

The Bible is a peculiar book. Words crafted in another language. Deeds done in a distant era. Events recorded in a far-off land. Counsel offered to a foreign people. It is a peculiar book.

It's surprising that anyone reads it. It's too old. Some of its writings date back five thousand years. It's too bizarre. The book speaks of incredible floods, fires, earthquakes, and people with supernatural abilities. It's too radical. The Bible calls for undying devotion to a carpenter who called himself God's Son.

Logic says this book shouldn't survive. Too old, too bizarre, too radical.

The Bible has been banned, burned, scoffed, and ridiculed. Scholars have mocked it as foolish. Kings have branded it as illegal. A thousand times over the grave has been dug and the dirge has begun, but somehow the Bible never stays in the grave. Not only has it survived, but it has also thrived. It is the single most popular book in all of history. It has been the bestselling book in the world for years!

There is no way on earth to explain it. Which perhaps is the only explanation. For the Bible's durability is not found on *earth* but in *heaven*. The millions who have tested its claims and claimed its promises know there is but one answer: the Bible is God's book and God's voice.

As you read it, you would be wise to give some thought to two questions: *What is the purpose of the Bible?* and *How do I study the Bible?* Time spent reflecting on these two issues will greatly enhance your Bible study.

What is the purpose of the Bible?

Let the Bible itself answer that question: "*From infancy you have known the Holy Scriptures, which are able to make you wise for salvation through faith in Christ Jesus*" (2 Timothy 3:15).

The purpose of the Bible? Salvation. God's highest passion is to get his children home. His book, the Bible, describes his plan of salvation. The purpose of the Bible is to proclaim God's plan and passion to save his children.

This is the reason why this book has endured through the centuries. It dares to tackle the toughest questions about life: *Where do I go after I die? Is there a God? What do I do with my fears?* The Bible is the treasure map that leads to God's highest treasure—eternal life.

But how do you study the Bible? Countless copies of Scripture sit unread on bookshelves and nightstands simply because people don't know how to read it. What can you do to make the Bible real in your life?

The clearest answer is found in the words of Jesus: "*Ask and it will be given to you; seek and you will find; knock and the door will be opened to you*" (Matthew 7:7).

The first step in understanding the Bible is asking God to help you. You should read it prayerfully. If anyone understands God's Word, it is because of God and not the reader.

"*The Advocate, the Holy Spirit, whom the Father will send in my name, will teach you all things and will remind you of everything I have said to you*" (John 14:26).

Before reading the Bible, pray and invite God to speak to you. Don't go to Scripture looking for your idea, but go searching for his.

Not only should you read the Bible prayerfully, but you should also read it carefully. "*Seek and you will find*" is the pledge. The Bible is not a newspaper to be skimmed but rather a mine to be quarried. "*If you look for it as for silver and search for it as for hidden treasure, then you will understand the fear of the LORD and find the knowledge of God*" (Proverbs 2:4–5).

Any worthy find requires effort. The Bible is no exception. To understand the Bible, you don't have to be brilliant, but you must be willing to roll up your sleeves and search.

"*Do your best to present yourself to God as one approved, a worker who does not need to be ashamed and who correctly handles the word of truth*" (2 Timothy 2:15).

Here's a practical point. Study the Bible a bit at a time. Hunger is not satisfied by eating twenty-one meals in one sitting once a week. The body needs a steady diet to remain strong. So does the soul. When God sent food to his people in the wilderness, he didn't provide loaves already made. Instead, he sent them manna in the shape of "*thin flakes like frost on the ground*" (Exodus 16:14).

God gave manna in limited portions.

God sends spiritual food the same way. He opens the heavens with just enough nutrients for today's hunger. He provides "*a rule for this, a rule for that; a little here, a little there*" (Isaiah 28:10).

Don't be discouraged if your reading reaps a small harvest. Some days a lesser portion is all that is needed. What is important is to search every day for that day's message. A steady diet of God's Word over a lifetime builds a healthy soul and mind.

It's much like the little girl who returned from her first day at school feeling a bit dejected. Her mom asked, "Did you learn anything?"

"Apparently not enough," the girl responded. "I have to go back tomorrow, and the next day, and the next . . . "

Such is the case with learning. And such is the case with Bible study. Understanding comes little by little over a lifetime.

There is a third step in understanding the Bible. After the asking and seeking comes the knocking. After you ask and search, "*knock and the door will be opened to you*" (Matthew 7:7).

To knock is to stand at God's door. To make yourself available. To climb the steps, cross the porch, stand at the doorway, and volunteer. Knocking goes beyond the realm of thinking and into the realm of acting.

To knock is to ask, *What can I do? How can I obey? Where can I go?*

It's one thing to know what to do. It's another to do it. But for those who do it—those who choose to obey—a special reward awaits them.

"*Whoever looks intently into the perfect law that gives freedom, and continues in it—not forgetting what they have heard, but doing it—they will be blessed in what they do*" (James 1:25).

What a promise. Blessings come to those who do what they read in God's Word! It's the same with medicine. If you only read the label but ignore the pills, it won't help. It's the same with food. If you only read the recipe but never cook, you won't be fed. And it's the same with the Bible. If you only read the words but never obey, you'll never know the joy God has promised.

Ask. Search. Knock. Simple, isn't it? So why don't you give it a try? If you do, you'll see why the Bible is the most remarkable book in history.

INTRODUCTION TO *The Book of 2 Samuel*

In the first ten chapters of 2 Samuel, David can do no wrong. He is never defeated in battle. Never wrong in judgment. He begins his reign in prayer (see 2:1) and continues in faith. Enemies are subdued, the nation is unified, the capital secured, and the boundary extends from six thousand to sixty thousand square miles.

You know what happened. On a lazy afternoon his wandering eyes found a forbidden maiden. Testosterone surged and evil urged, so he summoned her, slept with her, and then sent her home.

A rendezvous. So fast. So impulsive. So passionate. So pregnant.

Rather than repent, he connives and lies and leaves a soldier dead and a widow weeping and all of us wondering: *Is this the same David? Is this the shepherd? Is this the boy of faith? The man of prayer? Is this the man after God's own heart?*

With time, confession comes and forgiveness is given, but the scars remain. Nathan's prophecy proves true: The sword never departed from David's house (see 12:10). Bloodshed stained his home from then on.

Some of the final words written about David are some of the saddest: "King David was old, advanced in years; and they put covers on him, but he could not get warm" (1 Kings 1:1 NKJV).

Mark it down. Compromise chills the soul. If only David hadn't opened that cellar door.

AUTHOR AND DATE

The author of 1 and 2 Samuel (originally one book) is unknown, though Jewish tradition held it was written by Samuel himself along with the prophets Nathan and Gad (based on 1 Chronicles 29:29). Given that Samuel's death is recorded in 1 Samuel 25:1, he could only be the author of the first twenty-four chapters of that book, which means Nathan and Gad would have written all of 2 Samuel. A note in 1 Samuel 27:6 describing how the city of Ziklag was given "to the kings of Judah" seems to indicate the work was created after the rule of Solomon when the kingdom was divided between Israel and Judah in 931 BC. If this is the case—and the note was not added at a later time—it would rule out Samuel, Nathan, or Gad being the authors, as they all operated either before or during the rule of David. There is no clear indication as to how late the writing could be, but most likely it was penned before the exile, thus c. 931–722 BC.

SITUATION

The events in 2 Samuel begin after the deaths of Jonathan and Saul. At the time, David was in the city of Ziklag and learned the news from an Amalekite messenger who had escaped the Israelite camp. David's next move—after lamenting the deaths of both Jonathan and Saul—was to consolidate his position as king over Israel. This began with him first being anointed as king over Judah and then, after defeating Ish-Bosheth (a son of Saul), being anointed as king over all Israel. David's next move was to conquer Jerusalem, which he made into his capital, and bring the ark of the covenant there. He also made plans to build a "house" (temple) to the Lord, but God preempted these plans and promised to instead establish a "house" for him that would "endure forever" (7:16). Sadly, David's reign would be marred by an act of sin committed with a woman named Bathsheba and the murder of her husband. The action that follows in 2 Samuel covers the rest of what would be David's tumultuous reign, marked by internal strife within his family, a son attempting to usurp the throne, and David putting down other rebellions.

KEY THEMES

- Even though David had been mistreated by King Saul, he mourned Saul's passing.
- David was a man after God's own heart, a man of faith, even though he made mistakes.
- Among the good things David did, he returned the ark of the covenant to Jerusalem.
- Among the mistakes David made was his affair with Bathsheba and the resulting family discord.

KEY VERSE

"Your house and your kingdom shall be established forever before you. Your throne shall be established forever" (2 Samuel 7:16 NKJV).

CONTENTS

I. David's Kingdom (1:1–10:19)
II. David and Bathsheba (11:1–18:33)
III. David's Later Reign (19:1–24:25)

LESSON ONE

THE LOSS OF A FRIEND

They mourned and wept and fasted till evening for Saul and his son Jonathan.
2 SAMUEL 1:12

REFLECTION

How do you typically respond when you are confronted with loss?

SITUATION

The prophet Samuel had warned the Israelites that exchanging the Lord for a human king would bring consequences. Regardless, the people still cried out for a monarch, so God granted their request. Sadly, the prophet's words of warning proved to be well-founded. The people wanted a *leader*, but what they got was a *louse*. Saul, Israel's first king, was disobedient to God, which ultimately led to the Lord rejecting him. When this reality became apparent to Saul, he grew paranoid that a young warrior named David—who had recently won the people's hearts and minds because of his victory over the Philistine giant Goliath—would take his throne. Saul made David's life misery. He twice tried to end the young man's life by throwing a spear at him. David was forced to hide in caves and in enemy territory to escape Saul's wrath. This is where David was living—in the town of Ziklag given to him by the Philistine king Achish—when he learned that Jonathan, his dear friend, had fallen in battle and that Saul had taken his own life.

OBSERVATION

Read 2 Samuel 1:1–16 from the New International Version or the New King James Version.

New International Version

1 After the death of Saul, David returned from striking down the
Amalekites and stayed in Ziklag two days. 2 On the third day a man
arrived from Saul's camp with his clothes torn and dust on his head.
When he came to David, he fell to the ground to pay him honor.

3 "Where have you come from?" David asked him.

He answered, "I have escaped from the Israelite camp."

4 "What happened?" David asked. "Tell me."

"The men fled from the battle," he replied. "Many of them fell and died. And Saul and his son Jonathan are dead."

5 Then David said to the young man who brought him the report,
"How do you know that Saul and his son Jonathan are dead?"

6 "I happened to be on Mount Gilboa," the young man said, "and
there was Saul, leaning on his spear, with the chariots and their drivers
in hot pursuit. 7 When he turned around and saw me, he called out to me,
and I said, 'What can I do?'

8 "He asked me, 'Who are you?'

"'An Amalekite,' I answered.

9 "Then he said to me, 'Stand here by me and kill me! I'm in the
throes of death, but I'm still alive.'

10 "So I stood beside him and killed him, because I knew that after
he had fallen he could not survive. And I took the crown that was on his
head and the band on his arm and have brought them here to my lord."

11 Then David and all the men with him took hold of their clothes and tore them. 12 They mourned and wept and fasted till evening for Saul and his son Jonathan, and for the army of the LORD and for the nation of Israel, because they had fallen by the sword.

13 David said to the young man who brought him the report, "Where are you from?"

"I am the son of a foreigner, an Amalekite," he answered.

14 David asked him, "Why weren't you afraid to lift your hand to destroy the LORD's anointed?"

15 Then David called one of his men and said, "Go, strike him down!" So he struck him down, and he died. 16 For David had said to him, "Your blood be on your own head. Your own mouth testified against you when you said, 'I killed the LORD's anointed.'"

New King James Version

1 Now it came to pass after the death of Saul, when David had returned from the slaughter of the Amalekites, and David had stayed two days in Ziklag, 2 on the third day, behold, it happened that a man came from Saul's camp with his clothes torn and dust on his head. So it was, when he came to David, that he fell to the ground and prostrated himself.

3 And David said to him, "Where have you come from?"

So he said to him, "I have escaped from the camp of Israel."

4 Then David said to him, "How did the matter go? Please tell me."

And he answered, "The people have fled from the battle, many of the people are fallen and dead, and Saul and Jonathan his son are dead also."

5 So David said to the young man who told him, "How do you know that Saul and Jonathan his son are dead?"

6 Then the young man who told him said, "As I happened by chance to be on Mount Gilboa, there was Saul, leaning on his spear; and indeed the chariots and horsemen followed hard after him. 7 Now when he looked behind him, he saw me and called to me. And I answered, 'Here I am.' 8 And he said to me, 'Who are you?' So I answered him, 'I am an Amalekite.' 9 He said to me again, 'Please stand over me and kill me, for

anguish has come upon me, but my life still remains in me.' 10 So I stood
over him and killed him, because I was sure that he could not live after
he had fallen. And I took the crown that was on his head and the bracelet
that was on his arm, and have brought them here to my lord."

11 Therefore David took hold of his own clothes and tore them,
and so did all the men who were with him. 12 And they mourned and
wept and fasted until evening for Saul and for Jonathan his son, for the
people of the LORD and for the house of Israel, because they had fallen
by the sword.

13 Then David said to the young man who told him, "Where are
you from?"

And he answered, "I am the son of an alien, an Amalekite."

14 So David said to him, "How was it you were not afraid to put forth
your hand to destroy the LORD's anointed?" 15 Then David called one of
the young men and said, "Go near, and execute him!" And he struck him
so that he died. 16 So David said to him, "Your blood is on your own head,
for your own mouth has testified against you, saying, 'I have killed the
LORD's anointed.'"

EXPLORATION

1. What had David just returned from doing when the Amalekite messenger arrived?

2. How did the Amalekite messenger approach David? How did the man describe himself?

3. What did the Amalekite say about his encounter with King Saul on Mount Gilboa?

4. How did David and his men react to the news of the death of Saul and Jonathan?

5. What was David's question to the Amalekite messenger concerning the killing of Saul?

6. What does this story reveal about David's respect for Saul despite their past conflicts?

INSPIRATION

The giant of grief. We've felt his heavy hand on our shoulders. Not in Ziklag, but in emergency rooms, in children's hospitals, at car wrecks, and on battlefields. And we, like David, have two choices: Flee or face the giant.

Many opt to flee. The grave stirs such unspeakable hurt and unanswerable questions, we're tempted to turn and walk away. Change the subject, avoid the issue. Work hard. Drink harder. Stay busy. Stay distant. Yet we pay a high price when we do. Bereavement comes from the word *reave*. Look up *reave* in the dictionary, and you'll read "to take away by force, plunder, rob." Death robs you. The grave plunders moments and memories not yet shared: birthdays, vacations, lazy walks, talks over tea. We are bereaved because we've been robbed.

David, instead, chose to face his grief. Upon hearing of the deaths of Saul and Jonathan, "David lamented" (2 Samuel 1:17 NKJV). The warrior wept. The commander buried a bearded face in calloused hands and cried. He "ripped his clothes to ribbons. All the men with him did the same. They wept and fasted the rest of the day, grieving the death of Saul and his son Jonathan, and also the army of God and the nation Israel, victims in a failed battle" (verses 11–12 MSG).

Wailing warriors covered the hills, a herd of men walking, moaning, weeping, and mourning. They tore clothing, pounded the ground, and exhaled hurt. You need to do the same. Flush the hurt out of your heart, and when the hurt returns, flush it again.

Jesus did. Next to the tomb of his dear friend, "Jesus wept" (John 11:35). Why would he do such a thing? Did he not know of Lazarus's impending resurrection? He was one declaration from seeing his friend exit the grave. He'd see Lazarus before dinner. Why the tears?

Amid the answers we think we know and the many we don't is this one: Death stinks. Death amputates a limb of your life. So Jesus wept. And in his tears we find permission to shed our own. As the English pastor and evangelist F. B. Meyer once said, "Tears relieve the burning brain, as a shower in the electric clouds. Tears discharge the insupportable agony of the heart, as an overflow lessens the pressure of the flood against the dam. Tears are the material out of which heaven weaves its brightest rainbow." (From *Facing Your Giants* by Max Lucado.)

REACTION

7. David had the choice of *fleeing* or *facing* the giant of grief. What decision did he make? How do you think this choice benefitted him and the people of Israel?

8. *Bereavement* comes from the word *reave*. What does the definition of *reave* say about what death and loss do to a person?

9. Why was it important for David's warriors to "exhale" the hurt they felt at the loss of Saul and Jonathan? Why is it important for you to also "exhale" the hurt you feel?

10. What example did Jesus provide in how to face the loss of a friend?

11. What does F. B. Meyer say is the value of *tears* when it comes to grieving? In what ways are tears "the material out of which heaven weaves its brightest rainbow"?

12. Do you need to give yourself permission to grieve a loss? If so, what steps will you take to begin to face that loss rather than run from it?

LIFE LESSONS

When David learned of the death of Saul and Jonathan, he and his men tore their clothing, wept aloud, and fasted until sunset. His lament was intense: "Saul and Jonathan—in life they were loved and admired, and in death they were not parted" (2 Samuel 1:23). David not only sang this dirge but also ordered "the people of Judah be taught this lament" (verse 18). Denial and dismissal are not a part of God's grief therapy. Face it, fight it, question it, or condemn it, but don't deny it. As David's son Solomon would explain, "There is a time for everything . . . a time to weep . . . a time to mourn" (Ecclesiastes 3:1, 4). God will lead you through—not around—"the valley of the shadow of death" (Psalm 23:4 NKJV).

DEVOTION

Lord, I choose to acknowledge my grief and not run from it. Provide me with your comfort as I mourn this loss. Thank you for making a way, through the sacrifice of Jesus, for me to one day dwell with you in eternity.

JOURNALING

Who is someone you've lost who meant a great deal to you? Take a few moments to write out your own "song" that highlights some of your fondest memories of that person.

FOR FURTHER READING

To complete the book of 2 Samuel during this twelve-part study, read 2 Samuel 1:1–27. For more Bible passages about grief and sorrow, read Genesis 37:34–35; Psalm 34:18; 73:26; Ecclesiastes 7:3–4; Matthew 5:4; John 11:33–35; 1 Thessalonians 4:13; Revelation 21:4.

LESSON TWO

FOLLOWING GOD'S GUIDANCE

In the course of time, David inquired of the LORD. "Shall I go up to one of the towns of Judah?"
2 SAMUEL 2:1

REFLECTION

What steps do you take when you need guidance from the Lord?

SITUATION

David had recently returned from a successful campaign against the Amalekites when he received news that both Jonathan and Saul were dead. Ironically, the news came from an Amalekite messenger, who thought he would earn favor from David by claiming *he* was the one who had ended Saul's life. Instead, the Amalekite only earned David's wrath—and a death sentence—for striking down the Lord's anointed. David, overcome with grief, then composed a lament in honor of the fallen king and his son. Known as the "Song of the Bow," the elegy highlighted Saul's leadership and Jonathan's loyalty, describing them as mighty warriors whose deaths were a great tragedy and loss to the people of Israel. David commanded the song be taught to the people of Judah to ensure that Jonathan's and Saul's memories would endure. After this, David turned to the matter of finally assuming the throne over Israel.

OBSERVATION

Read 2 Samuel 2:1–17 from the New International Version or the New King James Version.

New International Version

[1] In the course of time, David inquired of the Lord. "Shall I go up to one of the towns of Judah?" he asked.

The Lord said, "Go up."

David asked, "Where shall I go?"

"To Hebron," the Lord answered.

[2] So David went up there with his two wives, Ahinoam of Jezreel and
Abigail, the widow of Nabal of Carmel. [3] David also took the men who
were with him, each with his family, and they settled in Hebron and its
towns. [4] Then the men of Judah came to Hebron, and there they anointed
David king over the tribe of Judah.

When David was told that it was the men from Jabesh Gilead who had buried Saul, [5] he sent messengers to them to say to them, "The LORD bless you for showing this kindness to Saul your master by burying him. [6] May the LORD now show you kindness and faithfulness, and I too will show you the same favor because you have done this. [7] Now then, be strong and brave, for Saul your master is dead, and the people of Judah have anointed me king over them."

[8] Meanwhile, Abner son of Ner, the commander of Saul's army, had taken Ish-Bosheth son of Saul and brought him over to Mahanaim. [9] He made him king over Gilead, Ashuri and Jezreel, and also over Ephraim, Benjamin and all Israel.

[10] Ish-Bosheth son of Saul was forty years old when he became king over Israel, and he reigned two years. The tribe of Judah, however, remained loyal to David. [11] The length of time David was king in Hebron over Judah was seven years and six months.

[12] Abner son of Ner, together with the men of Ish-Bosheth son of Saul, left Mahanaim and went to Gibeon. [13] Joab son of Zeruiah and David's men went out and met them at the pool of Gibeon. One group sat down on one side of the pool and one group on the other side.

[14] Then Abner said to Joab, "Let's have some of the young men get up and fight hand to hand in front of us."

"All right, let them do it," Joab said.

[15] So they stood up and were counted off—twelve men for Benjamin and Ish-Bosheth son of Saul, and twelve for David. [16] Then each man grabbed his opponent by the head and thrust his dagger into his opponent's side, and they fell down together. So that place in Gibeon was called Helkath Hazzurim.

[17] The battle that day was very fierce, and Abner and the Israelites were defeated by David's men.

NEW KING JAMES VERSION

[1] It happened after this that David inquired of the LORD, saying, "Shall I go up to any of the cities of Judah?"

And the LORD said to him, "Go up."

David said, "Where shall I go up?"

And He said, "To Hebron."

2 So David went up there, and his two wives also, Ahinoam the Jezreelitess, and Abigail the widow of Nabal the Carmelite. 3 And David brought up the men who were with him, every man with his household. So they dwelt in the cities of Hebron.

4 Then the men of Judah came, and there they anointed David king over the house of Judah. And they told David, saying, "The men of Jabesh Gilead were the ones who buried Saul." 5 So David sent messengers to the men of Jabesh Gilead, and said to them, "You are blessed of the LORD, for you have shown this kindness to your lord, to Saul, and have buried him. 6 And now may the LORD show kindness and truth to you. I also will repay you this kindness, because you have done this thing. 7 Now therefore, let your hands be strengthened, and be valiant; for your master Saul is dead, and also the house of Judah has anointed me king over them."

8 But Abner the son of Ner, commander of Saul's army, took Ishbosheth the son of Saul and brought him over to Mahanaim; 9 and he made him king over Gilead, over the Ashurites, over Jezreel, over Ephraim, over Benjamin, and over all Israel. 10 Ishbosheth, Saul's son, was forty years old when he began to reign over Israel, and he reigned two years. Only the house of Judah followed David. 11 And the time that David was king in Hebron over the house of Judah was seven years and six months.

12 Now Abner the son of Ner, and the servants of Ishbosheth the son of Saul, went out from Mahanaim to Gibeon. 13 And Joab the son of Zeruiah, and the servants of David, went out and met them by the pool of Gibeon. So they sat down, one on one side of the pool and the other on the other side of the pool. 14 Then Abner said to Joab, "Let the young men now arise and compete before us."

And Joab said, "Let them arise."

15 So they arose and went over by number, twelve from Benjamin, followers of Ishbosheth the son of Saul, and twelve from the servants of David. 16 And each one grasped his opponent by the head and thrust his

sword in his opponent's side; so they fell down together. Therefore that place was called the Field of Sharp Swords, which is in Gibeon. [17] So there was a very fierce battle that day, and Abner and the men of Israel were beaten before the servants of David.

EXPLORATION

1. What does the fact that David inquired of the Lord *before* going to the towns of Judah say about his desire to follow God's will?

2. What does this action on David's part reveal about his leadership?

3. How did the men of Judah show their support for David?

4. What did David say when he learned the men of Jabesh Gilead had buried Saul?

5. How did Abner's actions create division in Israel? What were the consequences of his actions?

6. How would you describe the battle that took place between the two sides at the pool of Gibeon?

INSPIRATION

David makes a habit of running his options past God. And he does so with a fascinating tool: the ephod. Trace its appearance to David's initial escape from Saul. David seeks comfort from the priests of Nob. Saul accuses the priests of harboring the fugitive, and, consistent with Saul's paranoia, he murders them. One priest by the name of Abiathar, however, flees. He escapes with more than just his life; he escapes with the ephod.

The ephod originated in the era of the wilderness wanderings. Moses presented the first one to Aaron, the priest. It was an ornate vest, woven of white linen, inwrought with threads of blue, purple, scarlet, and gold. A breastplate bearing twelve precious stones adorned the vest. The breastplate contained one or two, maybe three, resplendent diamonds or diamondlike stones. These stones had the names Urim and Thummim. No one knows the exact meaning of the terms, but "light" and "perfection" lead the list.

God revealed his will to the priests through these stones. How? Ancient writers have suggested several methods: the stones illuminated when God said yes, or contained moving letters that gathered to form a response, or were sacred lots that, upon being cast, would reveal an answer. While we speculate on the technique, we don't need to guess at the value. Would you not cherish such a tool? When faced with a puzzling choice, David could, with a reverent heart, make a request, and God would answer.

Will Saul come after me? He will.

Will the men capture me? They will.

Should I pursue the enemy? You should.

Will I overtake them? You will.

Oh, that God would do the same for us. That we could ask and he would answer. That we could cry out and he would reply. Wouldn't you love to have an ephod? Who's to say you don't? God hasn't changed. He still promises to guide us.

"I will instruct you and teach you in the way you should go; I will counsel you with my loving eye on you" (Psalm 32:8).

"In all your ways acknowledge Him, and He shall direct your paths" (Proverbs 3:6 NKJV).

"Whether you turn to the right or to the left, your ears will hear a voice behind you, saying, 'This is the way; walk in it' (Isaiah 30:21).

"My sheep listen to my voice; I know them, and they follow me" (John 10:27).

The God who guided David guides you. You simply need to consult your Maker. (From *Facing Your Giants* by Max Lucado.)

REACTION

7. What comes to mind when you picture the *ephod*? Why do you think God chose to reveal his will to the priests of Israel in this way?

8. David's requests to God were specific and direct. Does this match how you make your requests to God? What is the value in making specific requests?

9. Read James 1:5–6. What represents your *ephod* today? What is the promise contained in this passage for those who request God's wisdom?

10. What does Psalm 32:8 reveal about how God will guide you?

11. What does the Lord say in Isaiah 30:21 about how he will correct your steps?

12. What does it mean to "listen" to God's voice? What steps do you take to make sure you can recognize the voice of your Shepherd?

LIFE LESSONS

The road to kingship wasn't easy for David. After the death of Saul and Jonathan, only the tribe of Judah recognized him as their king. Eventually, after much strife, David would be recognized as king over *all* Israel. Yet even then, he recognized his reign had come about not as a result of anything *he* had done but because of what *God* had done. As he wrote, "[The Lord] gives his king great victories; he shows unfailing love to his anointed" (Psalm 18:50). God calls each of us to action and will work through our efforts to achieve his purposes on this earth. But ultimately, all the security and success we experience in this life comes solely from him. As David concluded, "Dominion belongs to the LORD and he rules over the nations" (Psalm 22:28).

DEVOTION

Heavenly Father, I look to you for guidance in my life. Forgive me for those times when I rush ahead and neglect to talk with you about my plans. I want to do everything according to your will and follow the steps that you have established for me. Thank you for giving me direction.

JOURNALING

What is something you are planning on doing but have neglected to bring before God? Take a few moments to write that below, and then write out your prayer asking for God's guidance.

FOR FURTHER READING

To complete the book of 2 Samuel during this twelve-part study, read 2 Samuel 2:1–3:39. For more Bible passages about God's guidance, read Psalm 32:8; Proverbs 3:5–6; 16:9; Isaiah 30:21; Matthew 6:33; John 16:13; Philippians 4:6; Hebrews 4:16.

LESSON THREE

OVERCOMING STRONGHOLDS

Nevertheless, David captured the fortress of Zion—which is the City of David.
2 Samuel 5:7

REFLECTION

What is a stronghold in your life that God has enabled you to overcome?

SITUATION

The people of Judah had anointed David as their king. However, the other tribes chose Ish-Bosheth, another son of Saul, to be their king. Ish-Bosheth had the backing of Abner, the commander of Saul's army, and war soon broke out between the houses. In one pitched battle, Abner killed the brother of Joab, the commander of David's army. Sometime later, Ish-Bosheth foolishly accused Abner of wrongdoing, prompting the general to switch sides. Joab, in turn, took the opportunity to avenge his brother's death by murdering Abner. David publicly mourned Abner's death, distancing himself from the act and earning the people's trust. Meanwhile, two of Ish-Bosheth's men murdered him and brought his head to David, expecting a reward. Instead, David condemned their treachery and had them executed. However, with Ish-Bosheth's death, the rest of the tribes were finally ready to accept David as their king.

OBSERVATION

Read 2 Samuel 5:1–25 from the New International Version or the New King James Version.

NEW INTERNATIONAL VERSION

1 All the tribes of Israel came to David at Hebron and said, "We are
your own flesh and blood. 2 In the past, while Saul was king over us,
you were the one who led Israel on their military campaigns. And the
LORD said to you, 'You will shepherd my people Israel, and you will
become their ruler.'"

3 When all the elders of Israel had come to King David at Hebron, the
king made a covenant with them at Hebron before the LORD, and they
anointed David king over Israel.

4 David was thirty years old when he became king, and he reigned
forty years. 5 In Hebron he reigned over Judah seven years and six
months, and in Jerusalem he reigned over all Israel and Judah thirty-
three years.

6 The king and his men marched to Jerusalem to attack the Jebusites,
who lived there. The Jebusites said to David, "You will not get in here;
even the blind and the lame can ward you off." They thought, "David
cannot get in here." 7 Nevertheless, David captured the fortress of Zion—
which is the City of David.

8 On that day David had said, "Anyone who conquers the Jebusites
will have to use the water shaft to reach those 'lame and blind' who are
David's enemies." That is why they say, "The 'blind and lame' will not
enter the palace."

9 David then took up residence in the fortress and called it the City of
David. He built up the area around it, from the terraces inward. 10 And
he became more and more powerful, because the LORD God Almighty
was with him.

11 Now Hiram king of Tyre sent envoys to David, along with cedar
logs and carpenters and stonemasons, and they built a palace for David.

12 Then David knew that the LORD had established him as king over Israel and had exalted his kingdom for the sake of his people Israel.

13 After he left Hebron, David took more concubines and wives in Jerusalem, and more sons and daughters were born to him. 14 These are the names of the children born to him there: Shammua, Shobab, Nathan, Solomon, 15 Ibhar, Elishua, Nepheg, Japhia, 16 Elishama, Eliada and Eliphelet.

17 When the Philistines heard that David had been anointed king over Israel, they went up in full force to search for him, but David heard about it and went down to the stronghold. 18 Now the Philistines had come and spread out in the Valley of Rephaim; 19 so David inquired of the LORD, "Shall I go and attack the Philistines? Will you deliver them into my hands?"

The LORD answered him, "Go, for I will surely deliver the Philistines into your hands."

20 So David went to Baal Perazim, and there he defeated them. He said, "As waters break out, the LORD has broken out against my enemies before me." So that place was called Baal Perazim. 21 The Philistines abandoned their idols there, and David and his men carried them off.

22 Once more the Philistines came up and spread out in the Valley of Rephaim; 23 so David inquired of the LORD, and he answered, "Do not go straight up, but circle around behind them and attack them in front of the poplar trees. 24 As soon as you hear the sound of marching in the tops of the poplar trees, move quickly, because that will mean the LORD has gone out in front of you to strike the Philistine army." 25 So David did as the LORD commanded him, and he struck down the Philistines all the way from Gibeon to Gezer.

New King James Version

1 Then all the tribes of Israel came to David at Hebron and spoke, saying, "Indeed we are your bone and your flesh. 2 Also, in time past, when Saul was king over us, you were the one who led Israel out and brought them in; and the LORD said to you, 'You shall shepherd My people Israel, and

be ruler over Israel.'" 3 Therefore all the elders of Israel came to the king at Hebron, and King David made a covenant with them at Hebron before the LORD. And they anointed David king over Israel. 4 David was thirty years old when he began to reign, and he reigned forty years. 5 In Hebron he reigned over Judah seven years and six months, and in Jerusalem he reigned thirty-three years over all Israel and Judah.

6 And the king and his men went to Jerusalem against the Jebusites, the inhabitants of the land, who spoke to David, saying, "You shall not come in here; but the blind and the lame will repel you," thinking, "David cannot come in here." 7 Nevertheless David took the stronghold of Zion (that is, the City of David).

8 Now David said on that day, "Whoever climbs up by way of the water shaft and defeats the Jebusites (the lame and the blind, who are hated by David's soul), he shall be chief and captain." Therefore they say, "The blind and the lame shall not come into the house."

9 Then David dwelt in the stronghold, and called it the City of David. And David built all around from the Millo and inward. 10 So David went on and became great, and the LORD God of hosts was with him.

11 Then Hiram king of Tyre sent messengers to David, and cedar trees, and carpenters and masons. And they built David a house. 12 So David knew that the LORD had established him as king over Israel, and that He had exalted His kingdom for the sake of His people Israel.

13 And David took more concubines and wives from Jerusalem, after he had come from Hebron. Also more sons and daughters were born to David. 14 Now these are the names of those who were born to him in Jerusalem: Shammua, Shobab, Nathan, Solomon, 15 Ibhar, Elishua, Nepheg, Japhia, 16 Elishama, Eliada, and Eliphelet.

17 Now when the Philistines heard that they had anointed David king over Israel, all the Philistines went up to search for David. And David heard of it and went down to the stronghold. 18 The Philistines also went and deployed themselves in the Valley of Rephaim. 19 So David inquired of the LORD, saying, "Shall I go up against the Philistines? Will You deliver them into my hand?"

And the LORD said to David, "Go up, for I will doubtless deliver the Philistines into your hand."

20 So David went to Baal Perazim, and David defeated them there; and he said, "The LORD has broken through my enemies before me, like a breakthrough of water." Therefore he called the name of that place
Baal Perazim. 21 And they left their images there, and David and his men carried them away.

22 Then the Philistines went up once again and deployed themselves
in the Valley of Rephaim. 23 Therefore David inquired of the LORD, and He said, "You shall not go up; circle around behind them, and come upon
them in front of the mulberry trees. 24 And it shall be, when you hear the sound of marching in the tops of the mulberry trees, then you shall advance quickly. For then the LORD will go out before you to strike the
camp of the Philistines." 25 And David did so, as the LORD commanded him; and he drove back the Philistines from Geba as far as Gezer.

EXPLORATION

1. Why did the tribes of Israel finally agree to recognize David as their rightful king?

2. What did the Jebusites say to discourage David from attacking the city of Jerusalem?

3. How did David and his army ultimately capture Jerusalem?

4. What actions did David take once the city was in his hands?

5. What did David do when he learned the Philistines were attacking?

6. How did the Lord instruct King David to conduct the second attack against the Philistines?

INSPIRATION

Strongholds: old, difficult, discouraging challenges. That's what David faced when he looked at Jerusalem. When you and I think of the city, we envision temples and prophets. We picture Jesus teaching, a New Testament church growing. We imagine a thriving, hub-of-history capital.

When David sees Jerusalem in 1000 BC, he sees something else. He sees a millennium-old, cheerless fortress, squatting defiantly on the spine of a ridge of hills. A rugged outcropping elevates her. Tall walls protect her. Jebusites indwell her. No one bothers them. Philistines fight the Amalekites. Amalekites fight the Hebrews. But the Jebusites? They are a coiled rattlesnake in the desert. Everyone leaves them alone.

Everyone, that is, except David.

The just-crowned king of Israel has his eye on Jerusalem. He's inherited a divided kingdom. The people need not just a strong leader but strong headquarters. David's present base of Hebron sits too far south to enlist the loyalties of the northern tribes. But if he moves north, he'll isolate the south. He seeks a neutral, centralized city. He wants Jerusalem.

We can only wonder how many times he's stared at her walls. He grew up in Bethlehem, only a day's walk to the south. He hid in the caves in the region of En Gedi, not far south. Surely he noticed Jerusalem. Somewhere he pegged the place as the perfect capital. The crown had scarcely been resized for his head when he set his eyes on his newest Goliath.

When David and men arrived at Jerusalem, the Jebusites said, "You shall not come in here; but the blind and the lame will repel you" (2 Samuel 5:6 NKJV). David ignored them and gave his instructions: "Anyone who conquers the Jebusites will have to use the water shaft to reach those 'lame and blind' who are David's enemies" (verse 8). The result? "Then David dwelt in the stronghold, and called it the City of David" (verse 9 NKJV).

This regrettably brief story tantalizes us with the appearance of the term *stronghold*. Jerusalem met the qualifications of one: an old, difficult, and discouraging fortress. From atop the turrets, Jebusite soldiers had ample time to direct arrows at any would-be wall climbers. And discouraging? Just look at how the city-dwellers taunted David.

"Nevertheless David took the stronghold of Zion" (verse 7 NKJV). If you've heard the mocking David heard, then your story needs the word David's has. Did you see it? Most hurry past it. Let's not. Pull out a pen and underline this twelve-letter masterpiece.

Nevertheless.

"Nevertheless David took the stronghold." We all need a *nevertheless*. And God has plenty to go around. Strongholds mean nothing to him. As Paul wrote, "We use God's mighty weapons, not mere worldly weapons, to knock down the Devil's strongholds" (2 Corinthians 10:4 NLT). What God did for David he can do for us. (From *Facing Your Giants* by Max Lucado.)

REACTION

7. Why did David want to make Jerusalem his headquarters? What overall purpose did it serve in his plans to lead a united Israel?

8. What made the Jebusites feel secure enough behind their walls to taunt David? What daunting task did David and his men face when setting out to displace them?

9. How would you define what a *stronghold* looks like in your life?

10. What is the significance of the word *nevertheless* in David's story? What would you say is the significance of this word when it comes to the strongholds in your life?

11. What does Paul say in 2 Corinthians 10:4 about the weapons you have been given to knock down the enemy's strongholds?

12. Are you consistently and actively using these weapons from God? If not, what steps do you need to take today to start using them?

LIFE LESSONS

Two types of thoughts vie for your attention. One says, *Yes you can.* The other says, *No you can't.* One says, *God will help you.* The other lies, *God has left you.* One speaks the language of heaven; the other deceives in the vernacular of the Jebusites. One proclaims God's strengths; the other lists your failures. One longs to build you up; the other seeks to tear you down. And here's the great news: You get to select the voice you hear. So why listen to the mockers? Why heed their voices? Why give ear to critics and scoffers when you can, with the same ear, listen to the voice of God? You can do what David did. You can turn a deaf ear to old voices.

DEVOTION

Lord, I choose to pick up the weapons you have provided that have divine power to demolish strongholds. Help me to wield these weapons effectively as I break down any footholds the enemy has established in my life. Thank you, heavenly Father, for your continual mercy.

JOURNALING

What are some of the negative thoughts the enemy is trying to plant in your mind? Write these out below, and then write out how God would want you to counter these thoughts.

FOR FURTHER READING

To complete the book of 2 Samuel during this twelve-part study, read 2 Samuel 4:1–5:25. For more Bible passages about overcoming sin and strongholds, read Psalm 103:2–4; 119:11; Isaiah 54:17; 2 Corinthians 10:5; Galatians 5:1; Ephesians 6:13; James 4:7; 1 John 1:9.

LESSON FOUR

GOD COMES ON HIS TERMS

The Lord's anger burned against Uzzah because of his irreverent act; therefore God struck him down, and he died there beside the ark of God.
2 Samuel 6:7

REFLECTION

What are some of the consequences you have seen when people do not follow God's instructions?

SITUATION

David's first act after becoming king over all Israel was to take Jerusalem from the Jebusites. He accomplished this feat by sending soldiers through the city's water shaft to capture it from the inside out. Once the city was secured, David made it into his capital, fortifying the area around it and having his palace built there (with assistance from the king of Tyre). David's power and influence continued to grow, leading him to take more wives and concubines and to father many more children. In time, the Philistines learned of David's anointing as king over Israel and launched two attacks against him. In the first battle at Baal Perazim, the Lord broke through Israel's enemies like a flood and gave them the victory. In the second battle at the Valley of Rephaim, David followed God's instructions to have his forces circle behind the Philistines, and the Israelites won that battle as well. After these two decisive victories, David turned to another matter that had evidently been on his heart.

OBSERVATION

Read 2 Samuel 6:1–19 from the New International Version or the New King James Version.

New International Version

[1] David again brought together all the able young men of Israel—thirty
thousand. [2] He and all his men went to Baalah in Judah to bring up from
there the ark of God, which is called by the Name, the name of the Lord
Almighty, who is enthroned between the cherubim on the ark. [3] They set
the ark of God on a new cart and brought it from the house of Abinadab,
which was on the hill. Uzzah and Ahio, sons of Abinadab, were guiding
the new cart [4] with the ark of God on it, and Ahio was walking in front
of it. [5] David and all Israel were celebrating with all their might before
the Lord, with castanets, harps, lyres, timbrels, sistrums and cymbals.

[6] When they came to the threshing floor of Nakon, Uzzah reached
out and took hold of the ark of God, because the oxen stumbled. [7] The
Lord's anger burned against Uzzah because of his irreverent act; therefore God struck him down, and he died there beside the ark of God.

[8] Then David was angry because the Lord's wrath had broken out
against Uzzah, and to this day that place is called Perez Uzzah.

[9] David was afraid of the Lord that day and said, "How can the ark
of the Lord ever come to me?" [10] He was not willing to take the ark of the
Lord to be with him in the City of David. Instead, he took it to the house

of Obed-Edom the Gittite. [11] The ark of the LORD remained in the house of Obed-Edom the Gittite for three months, and the LORD blessed him and his entire household.

[12] Now King David was told, "The LORD has blessed the household of Obed-Edom and everything he has, because of the ark of God." So David went to bring up the ark of God from the house of Obed-Edom to the City of David with rejoicing. [13] When those who were carrying the ark of the LORD had taken six steps, he sacrificed a bull and a fattened calf. [14] Wearing a linen ephod, David was dancing before the LORD with all his might, [15] while he and all Israel were bringing up the ark of the LORD with shouts and the sound of trumpets.

[16] As the ark of the LORD was entering the City of David, Michal daughter of Saul watched from a window. And when she saw King David leaping and dancing before the LORD, she despised him in her heart.

[17] They brought the ark of the LORD and set it in its place inside the tent that David had pitched for it, and David sacrificed burnt offerings and fellowship offerings before the LORD. [18] After he had finished sacrificing the burnt offerings and fellowship offerings, he blessed the people in the name of the LORD Almighty. [19] Then he gave a loaf of bread, a cake of dates and a cake of raisins to each person in the whole crowd of Israelites, both men and women. And all the people went to their homes.

NEW KING JAMES VERSION

[1] Again David gathered all the choice men of Israel, thirty thousand. [2] And David arose and went with all the people who were with him from Baale Judah to bring up from there the ark of God, whose name is called by the Name, the LORD of Hosts, who dwells between the cherubim. [3] So they set the ark of God on a new cart, and brought it out of the house of Abinadab, which was on the hill; and Uzzah and Ahio, the sons of Abinadab, drove the new cart. [4] And they brought it out of the house of Abinadab, which was on the hill, accompanying the ark of God; and Ahio went before the ark. [5] Then David and all the house of Israel played

music before the LORD on all kinds of instruments of fir wood, on harps,
on stringed instruments, on tambourines, on sistrums, and on cymbals.

6 And when they came to Nachon's threshing floor, Uzzah put out
his hand to the ark of God and took hold of it, for the oxen stumbled. 7
Then the anger of the LORD was aroused against Uzzah, and God struck
him there for his error; and he died there by the ark of God. 8 And David
became angry because of the LORD's outbreak against Uzzah; and he
called the name of the place Perez Uzzah to this day.

9 David was afraid of the LORD that day; and he said, "How can the
ark of the LORD come to me?" 10 So David would not move the ark of the
LORD with him into the City of David; but David took it aside into the
house of Obed-Edom the Gittite. 11 The ark of the LORD remained in the
house of Obed-Edom the Gittite three months. And the LORD blessed
Obed-Edom and all his household.

12 Now it was told King David, saying, "The LORD has blessed the
house of Obed-Edom and all that belongs to him, because of the ark of
God." So David went and brought up the ark of God from the house of
Obed-Edom to the City of David with gladness. 13 And so it was, when
those bearing the ark of the LORD had gone six paces, that he sacrificed
oxen and fatted sheep. 14 Then David danced before the LORD with all
his might; and David was wearing a linen ephod. 15 So David and all the
house of Israel brought up the ark of the LORD with shouting and with
the sound of the trumpet.

16 Now as the ark of the LORD came into the City of David, Michal,
Saul's daughter, looked through a window and saw King David leaping
and whirling before the LORD; and she despised him in her heart. 17 So
they brought the ark of the LORD, and set it in its place in the midst of
the tabernacle that David had erected for it. Then David offered burnt
offerings and peace offerings before the LORD. 18 And when David had
finished offering burnt offerings and peace offerings, he blessed the
people in the name of the LORD of hosts. 19 Then he distributed among
all the people, among the whole multitude of Israel, both the women and

the men, to everyone a loaf of bread, a piece of meat, and a cake of raisins. So all the people departed, everyone to his house.

EXPLORATION

1. Read Numbers 7:6–9. What fundamental error did David and the people make the first time they decided to bring the ark to Jerusalem?

2. Now read Numbers 4:15. How does this command from the Lord explain why Uzzah died when he reached out to steady the ark?

3. What was David's reaction when Uzzah was struck down?

4. What indicated to David—after this disastrous first attempt—that it was time to again make plans to bring the ark to Jerusalem?

5. What did David and the people do differently on this second attempt?

6. How did Michal respond when she saw David dancing before the Lord? What does this reveal about her heart and her attitude toward him?

INSPIRATION

They gather near the home of Abinadab, the priest. His two sons, Uzzah and Ahio, are put in charge of the transport. They load the ark on an ox-drawn wagon and begin the march.

Trumpets blast, songs erupt, and all goes well for the first two miles, until they hit a patch of rough road. The oxen stumble, the wagon shakes, and the ark shifts. Uzzah, thinking the holy chest is about to fall off the wagon, extends his hand to steady it. And heaven Uzi-ed Uzzah, and "and he died there" (2 Samuel 6:7).

This will dampen a parade real quick. Everyone goes home. Deeply distressed, David returns to Jerusalem. The ark is kept at the home of Obed-Edom while David sorts things out. Apparently, he succeeds, because at the end of three months David returns, reclaims the ark, and resumes the parade. This time there is no death. There is dancing. David enters Jerusalem with rejoicing. And "David danced before the LORD with all his might" (verse 14 NKJV).

Two men. One dead. The other dancing. What do they teach us? Specifically, what do they teach us about invoking the presence of God?

This is what David wants to know: "How can the ark of the LORD ever come to me?" (verse 9).

In the story of David and his giants, this is one giant-size issue. Is God a distant deity? Mothers ask, "How can the presence of God come over my children?" Fathers ponder, "How can God's presence fill my house?" Churches desire the touching, helping, healing presence of God in their midst.

How can the presence of God come to us?

Should we light a candle, sing chants, build an altar, head up a committee, give a barrelful of money? What invokes the presence of God? Uzzah and David blend death and dancing to reveal an answer.

Uzzah's tragedy teaches this: *God comes on his own terms.* He gave specific instructions as to the care and transport of the ark. Only the priests could draw near it. And then only after they had offered sacrifices for themselves and their families.

The image of a dead Uzzah sends a sobering and shuddering reminder to those of us who can attend church as often as we wish, take communion anytime we desire. The message: Don't grow lax before the holy. God won't be loaded on convenient wagons or toted about by dumb animals. Don't confuse him with a genie who pops out at the rub of a lamp or a butler who appears at the ring of a bell.

God comes, mind you. But he comes on his own terms. (From *Facing Your Giants* by Max Lucado.)

REACTION

7. "The fear of the LORD is the beginning of knowledge" (Proverbs 1:7). What does it mean to *fear* the Lord? How does this lead to wisdom?

8. Why do you think God established certain rules for how his people could approach him?

9. What does Uzzah's tragedy reveal about the dangers in coming to God on *your* terms?

10. How does Uzzah's story challenge you to reflect on areas where you might have grown too casual or lax in your faith?

11. Why was David's "leaping and dancing" (2 Samuel 6:16) an appropriate act of worship? How do you balance reverence for God with the joy of celebrating his presence?

12. In what way would you like God to make his presence known in your life today?

LIFE LESSONS

"Get a new cart ready, with two cows that have calved and have never been yoked. . . . Take the ark of the LORD and put it on the cart" (1 Samuel 6:7–8). When the Israelites set out to bring the ark to Jerusalem, they moved it in the same way the Philistines had moved it. God's people knew better. They had the Law of Moses to guide them on the proper way to transport the ark—and they were responsible for obeying those rules that God had established. Jesus said, "God is spirit, and his worshipers must worship in the Spirit and in truth" (John 4:24). As God's people, we worship him based on the truth of God's Word and with a spirit that longs to obey his commands. We cannot grow lax before the holy.

DEVOTION

God, forgive me for those times when I am lax in the honor and respect that I show to you. Help me to remember that you are holy and to never take your mercy toward me for granted. I desire to be obedient in all areas of my life and seek to live up to your high calling for me.

JOURNALING

What is it that strikes awe in you when you consider God's greatness and his incredible acts of mercy? Take a few minutes to write out a few things for which you are especially grateful.

FOR FURTHER READING

To complete the book of 2 Samuel during this twelve-part study, read 2 Samuel 6:1–23. For more Bible passages about the fear of the Lord, read Deuteronomy 10:12; Job 28:28; Psalm 111:10; Proverbs 8:13; Ecclesiastes 12:13; Luke 1:50; 2 Corinthians 7:1; Hebrews 12:28.

LESSON FIVE

AN ETERNAL COVENANT

"When your days are over and you rest with your ancestors, I will raise up your offspring to succeed you, your own flesh and blood, and I will establish his kingdom."

2 Samuel 7:12

REFLECTION

What helps you to know that God always keeps his promises?

SITUATION

David could not contain his exuberance when the ark was brought into Jerusalem. Donning a linen ephod, a simple garment worn by priests, he danced before the Lord as the procession made its way into the city. Meanwhile, David's wife Michal, the daughter of Saul, watched him from a window. When the king returned home to bless his household, she criticized him for his "vulgar" behavior. David quickly defended his actions, declaring that he would become even *more* undignified in his worship of the Lord. Sadly, Michal would have "no children to the day of her death" (2 Samuel 6:23). After this, as David settled into his palace, he began to feel it was inappropriate for the ark to remain in a simple tent while he lived in a house of cedar. So he reached out to a prophet named Nathan to share his plan to remedy the situation.

OBSERVATION

Read 2 Samuel 7:1–17 from the New International Version or the New King James Version.

New International Version

1 After the king was settled in his palace and the Lord had given him rest
from all his enemies around him, 2 he said to Nathan the prophet, "Here
I am, living in a house of cedar, while the ark of God remains in a tent."

3 Nathan replied to the king, "Whatever you have in mind, go ahead
and do it, for the Lord is with you."

4 But that night the word of the Lord came to Nathan, saying:

5 "Go and tell my servant David, 'This is what the Lord says: Are you
the one to build me a house to dwell in? 6 I have not dwelt in a house from
the day I brought the Israelites up out of Egypt to this day. I have been
moving from place to place with a tent as my dwelling. 7 Wherever I have
moved with all the Israelites, did I ever say to any of their rulers whom I
commanded to shepherd my people Israel, "Why have you not built me
a house of cedar?"'

8 "Now then, tell my servant David, 'This is what the Lord Almighty
says: I took you from the pasture, from tending the flock, and appointed
you ruler over my people Israel. 9 I have been with you wherever you have
gone, and I have cut off all your enemies from before you. Now I will
make your name great, like the names of the greatest men on earth. 10

And I will provide a place for my people Israel and will plant them so that
they can have a home of their own and no longer be disturbed. Wicked
people will not oppress them anymore, as they did at the beginning 11
and have done ever since the time I appointed leaders over my people
Israel. I will also give you rest from all your enemies.

"'The LORD declares to you that the LORD himself will establish a
house for you: 12 When your days are over and you rest with your ancestors, I will raise up your offspring to succeed you, your own flesh and
blood, and I will establish his kingdom. 13 He is the one who will build a
house for my Name, and I will establish the throne of his kingdom forever. 14 I will be his father, and he will be my son. When he does wrong,
I will punish him with a rod wielded by men, with floggings inflicted
by human hands. 15 But my love will never be taken away from him, as I
took it away from Saul, whom I removed from before you. 16 Your house
and your kingdom will endure forever before me; your throne will be
established forever.'"

17 Nathan reported to David all the words of this entire revelation.

NEW KING JAMES VERSION

1 Now it came to pass when the king was dwelling in his house, and the
LORD had given him rest from all his enemies all around, 2 that the king
said to Nathan the prophet, "See now, I dwell in a house of cedar, but the
ark of God dwells inside tent curtains."

3 Then Nathan said to the king, "Go, do all that is in your heart, for
the LORD is with you."

4 But it happened that night that the word of the LORD came to
Nathan, saying, 5 "Go and tell My servant David, 'Thus says the LORD:
"Would you build a house for Me to dwell in? 6 For I have not dwelt in a
house since the time that I brought the children of Israel up from Egypt,
even to this day, but have moved about in a tent and in a tabernacle. 7
Wherever I have moved about with all the children of Israel, have I ever
spoken a word to anyone from the tribes of Israel, whom I commanded
to shepherd My people Israel, saying, 'Why have you not built Me a house

of cedar?”’” 8 Now therefore, thus shall you say to My servant David,
‘Thus says the LORD of hosts: “I took you from the sheepfold, from following the sheep, to be ruler over My people, over Israel. 9 And I have
been with you wherever you have gone, and have cut off all your enemies
from before you, and have made you a great name, like the name of the
great men who are on the earth. 10 Moreover I will appoint a place for My
people Israel, and will plant them, that they may dwell in a place of their
own and move no more; nor shall the sons of wickedness oppress them
anymore, as previously, 11 since the time that I commanded judges to be
over My people Israel, and have caused you to rest from all your enemies.
Also the LORD tells you that He will make you a house.

12 “When your days are fulfilled and you rest with your fathers, I
will set up your seed after you, who will come from your body, and I will
establish his kingdom. 13 He shall build a house for My name, and I will
establish the throne of his kingdom forever. 14 I will be his Father, and he
shall be My son. If he commits iniquity, I will chasten him with the rod
of men and with the blows of the sons of men. 15 But My mercy shall not
depart from him, as I took it from Saul, whom I removed from before
you. 16 And your house and your kingdom shall be established forever
before you. Your throne shall be established forever.”’”

17 According to all these words and according to all this vision, so
Nathan spoke to David.

EXPLORATION

1. What made David feel unsettled about the ark just being in a tent?

2. What was Nathan's initial response to David's desire to build a house for the Lord?

3. What did God say (through Nathan) about his dwelling place among the Israelites?

4. What promise did the Lord make to David about how his name would be regarded in history? What promise did God make concerning a place for his people?

5. What promise did the Lord make about David's descendants and his kingdom?

6. What does this story reveal about how God responds to those have a heart for him?

INSPIRATION

My dad made a big deal out of family vacations. Our holidays always consisted of a long road trip that began at our home in West Texas and ended up in a campground. Weeks before we left, he would start planning the itinerary. He had no internet or GPS; he planned his trips using a map. He traced out the journey with a highlighter. He circled the campgrounds and made notes of the highway numbers. Once he had his plans, he shared them with us.

My brother and I were just kids, single digits in age and inexperienced in the ways of the road. So Dad would sit with us at the table, show us the map, and tell us what to expect.

"Boys, we leave next week for the Grand Canyon. Let me tell you all the things we will do." Trout fishing. Tent camping. Marshmallow melting. Whitewater rafting.

My brother and I grew saucer-eyed. We had every reason to do so. When Dad said we would do something, we always did it. It was as good as done.

Dad told us his plans and what to expect. Our heavenly Father has also done that. Want to know what he has in store for humanity? Start in the garden of Eden. God revealed our destination in creation. But don't stop there. Next get acquainted with his covenants.

A covenant is a contract, treaty, agreement, or alliance between two parties. It formally binds the two parties in a relationship. Our God is a covenant-making and covenant-*keeping* God. He is not like us. We remake our decisions and reconsider our opinions. We are prone to make a promise only to break it due to unforeseen circumstances. Not God. His decrees are not his *desire* for the future. They are his *description* of the future.

God made a covenant with David: "When your days are over and you rest with your ancestors, I will raise up your offspring to succeed you, your own flesh and blood, and I will establish his kingdom. . . . Your house and your kingdom will endure forever before me; your throne will be established forever" (2 Samuel 7:12, 16). The Lord declared that someone from the house of David would sit on David's throne and rule over his kingdom forever.

About a thousand years later, the angel Gabriel quoted this covenant to a young Hebrew girl named Mary: "He will be great, and will be called the Son of the Highest, and the Lord God will give Him the throne of His father David. And He will reign over the house of Jacob forever, and of His kingdom there will be no end" (Luke 1:32–33 NKJV).

Jesus was this promised future descendant of David. He would establish a new kingdom on earth—the kingdom of God, which would endure forever. God kept his promises to David, just as he keeps his promises to us today. (From *What Happens Next* by Max Lucado.)

REACTION

7. What does the story of creation—particularly Adam and Eve in the garden of Eden—reveal about the destination that God has for his people?

8. What is the definition of a *covenant*? What does a covenant do between the parties?

9. What is the difference between the covenants that God makes with people and the covenants that people make among themselves?

10. What does God's covenant with David reveal about his faithfulness to his people?

11. In what ways was Jesus the fulfillment of the promise that God had made to David?

12. How does knowing that God's nature is unchanging encourage you to trust in him?

LIFE LESSONS

"But that night the word of the LORD came to Nathan" (2 Samuel 7:4). Many of the promises God made in this "word" were fulfilled during or shortly after David's reign. God promised, "I will raise up your offspring to succeed you" (verse 12), and this was fulfilled in Solomon. God promised, "I will provide a place for my people Israel" (verse 10), and this was true for the Israelites during David's lifetime. But God also promised to establish David's throne and kingdom *forever*, which extended beyond David's lifetime. Jesus, a future descendant of David—his "own flesh and blood" (verse 12)—would be the fulfillment of this promise. He would establish a kingdom "not of this world" but an eternal kingdom "from another place" (John 18:36). God kept *all* of his promises to David.

DEVOTION

Father, thank you for being a covenant-keeping God. I can always rely on the promises in your Word because your nature never changes. Help me to model the faithfulness that you show toward me toward others.

JOURNALING

What has God done in the past that helps you to entrust your future to him? Take a few minutes today to write down whatever comes to mind.

FOR FURTHER READING

To complete the book of 2 Samuel during this twelve-part study, read 2 Samuel 7:1–8:18. For more Bible passages about God's promises to his people, read Deuteronomy 31:8; Joshua 23:14; Isaiah 41:10; Jeremiah 29:11; John 14:3; 2 Corinthians 1:20; Philippians 4:19; 2 Peter 1:4.

LESSON SIX

A PROMISE TO KEEP

The king asked, "Is there no one still alive from the house of Saul to whom I can show God's kindness?"
2 Samuel 9:3

REFLECTION

What is the toughest promise that you've had to keep in your life?

SITUATION

David had wanted to build a house for the Lord, but God revealed that he would instead build a house for David—a covenant promise to establish his kingdom *forever.* David responded by humbly going before the Lord and sitting in his presence. He marveled at God's blessings, expressed his awe that the Lord would establish the Israelites as his people, prayed for the fulfillment of these promises, and asked God to continue to bless his house. After this, David won victories over the Philistines, Moabites, Arameans, and Edomites, which expanded Israel's territory and brought wealth into the kingdom. Now, with the nation secure, David wondered if there was anyone left in Saul's house to whom he could show kindness for Jonathan's sake.

OBSERVATION

Read 2 Samuel 9:1–13 from the New International Version or the New King James Version.

NEW INTERNATIONAL VERSION

1 David asked, "Is there anyone still left of the house of Saul to whom I can show kindness for Jonathan's sake?"

2 Now there was a servant of Saul's household named Ziba. They summoned him to appear before David, and the king said to him, "Are you Ziba?"

"At your service," he replied.

3 The king asked, "Is there no one still alive from the house of Saul to whom I can show God's kindness?"

Ziba answered the king, "There is still a son of Jonathan; he is lame in both feet."

4 "Where is he?" the king asked.

Ziba answered, "He is at the house of Makir son of Ammiel in Lo Debar."

5 So King David had him brought from Lo Debar, from the house of Makir son of Ammiel.

6 When Mephibosheth son of Jonathan, the son of Saul, came to David, he bowed down to pay him honor.

David said, "Mephibosheth!"

"At your service," he replied.

[7] "Don't be afraid," David said to him, "for I will surely show you kindness for the sake of your father Jonathan. I will restore to you all the land that belonged to your grandfather Saul, and you will always eat at my table."

[8] Mephibosheth bowed down and said, "What is your servant, that you should notice a dead dog like me?"

[9] Then the king summoned Ziba, Saul's steward, and said to him, "I have given your master's grandson everything that belonged to Saul and
his family. [10] You and your sons and your servants are to farm the land for him and bring in the crops, so that your master's grandson may be provided for. And Mephibosheth, grandson of your master, will always eat at my table." (Now Ziba had fifteen sons and twenty servants.)

[11] Then Ziba said to the king, "Your servant will do whatever my lord the king commands his servant to do." So Mephibosheth ate at David's table like one of the king's sons.

[12] Mephibosheth had a young son named Mika, and all the members
of Ziba's household were servants of Mephibosheth. [13] And Mephibosheth
lived in Jerusalem, because he always ate at the king's table; he was lame in both feet.

New King James Version

[1] Now David said, "Is there still anyone who is left of the house of Saul, that I may show him kindness for Jonathan's sake?"

[2] And there was a servant of the house of Saul whose name was Ziba. So when they had called him to David, the king said to him, "Are you Ziba?"

He said, "At your service!"

[3] Then the king said, "Is there not still someone of the house of Saul, to whom I may show the kindness of God?"

And Ziba said to the king, "There is still a son of Jonathan who is lame in his feet."

[4] So the king said to him, "Where is he?"

And Ziba said to the king, "Indeed he is in the house of Machir the son of Ammiel, in Lo Debar."

[5] Then King David sent and brought him out of the house of Machir the son of Ammiel, from Lo Debar.

[6] Now when Mephibosheth the son of Jonathan, the son of Saul, had come to David, he fell on his face and prostrated himself. Then David said, "Mephibosheth?"

And he answered, "Here is your servant!"

[7] So David said to him, "Do not fear, for I will surely show you kindness for Jonathan your father's sake, and will restore to you all the land of Saul your grandfather; and you shall eat bread at my table continually."

[8] Then he bowed himself, and said, "What is your servant, that you should look upon such a dead dog as I?"

[9] And the king called to Ziba, Saul's servant, and said to him, "I have given to your master's son all that belonged to Saul and to all his house.
[10] You therefore, and your sons and your servants, shall work the land for him, and you shall bring in the harvest, that your master's son may have food to eat. But Mephibosheth your master's son shall eat bread at my table always." Now Ziba had fifteen sons and twenty servants.

[11] Then Ziba said to the king, "According to all that my lord the king has commanded his servant, so will your servant do."

"As for Mephibosheth," said the king, "he shall eat at my table like
one of the king's sons." [12] Mephibosheth had a young son whose name
was Micha. And all who dwelt in the house of Ziba were servants of
Mephibosheth. [13] So Mephibosheth dwelt in Jerusalem, for he ate continually at the king's table. And he was lame in both his feet.

EXPLORATION

1. Read 1 Samuel 20:14–17. What promise did David make to Jonathan?

2. At this point in David's reign, "the LORD had given him rest from all his enemies" (2 Samuel 7:1). How might this have led to him remembering this promise to Jonathan?

3. Review 2 Samuel 4:4. How did Ziba describe Mephibosheth's condition? What had led to Mephibosheth being in this state?

4. What promises did David make to Mephibosheth when they met?

5. How did Mephibosheth respond to David's kindness?

6. What instructions did David give to Ziba concerning Mephibosheth?

INSPIRATION

King David's life couldn't be better. Just crowned. His throne room smells like fresh paint, and his city architect is laying out new neighborhoods. God's ark indwells the tabernacle; gold and silver overflow the king's coffers; Israel's enemies maintain their distance. The days of ducking Saul are a distant memory.

But something stirs one of them. A comment, perhaps, resurrects an old conversation. Maybe a familiar face jars a dated decision. In the midst of his new life, David remembers a promise from his old one: "Is there anyone still left of the house of Saul to whom I can show kindness for Jonathan's sake?" (2 Samuel 9:1).

Confusion furrows the faces of David's court. Why bother with the children of Saul? This is a new era, a new administration. Who cares about the old guard? David does. He does because he remembers the covenant that he made with Jonathan. When Saul threatened to kill him, Jonathan sought to save him. Jonathan succeeded and then made this request: "If I make it through this alive, continue to be my covenant friend. And if I die, keep the covenant friendship with my family—forever" (1 Samuel 20:14–15 MSG).

Jonathan does die. But David's covenant does not. And to him, a covenant was no small matter. Of course, finding a descendant of Jonathan wouldn't be easy. No one in David's circle knew one. So his advisers summoned Ziba, a former servant of Saul. Did he know of a surviving member of Saul's household?

Take a good look at Ziba's answer: "There is still a son of Jonathan; he is lame in both feet" (verse 3). Ziba gives no details about the boy, but in 2 Samuel 4:4, we learn that his name is Mephibosheth. (What great names! Needing ideas on what to name your newborns? Try Ziba and Mephibosheth. They'll stand out in their class.)

When Mephibosheth was five, his father and grandfather died at the hands of the Philistines. Knowing their brutality, Saul's family headed for the hills. Mephibosheth's nurse snatched him up and ran, then tripped and dropped the boy, breaking both his ankles, leaving him incurably lame. Escaping servants carried him across the Jordan River to an inhospitable village called Lo Debar. The name means "without pasture."

Picture a tumbleweed-tossed, low-rent trailer town in an Arizona desert. Mephibosheth hid there, first for fear of the Philistines, then for fear of David.

Victimized. Ostracized. Disabled. Uncultured. "Are you sure?" Ziba's reply insinuates, "Are you sure you want the likes of this boy in your palace?" David is sure. Faster than you can say "Mephibosheth" twice, he gets promoted from Lo Debar to the king's table.

David would not break his promise to Jonathan. In the same way, God will never break his promise to you. Your eternal life is covenant caused, covenant secured, and covenant based. You can put Lo Debar in the rearview mirror for one reason—God keeps his promises. (From *Facing Your Giants* by Max Lucado.)

REACTION

7. Saul had spent years trying to kill David. Given this, why would it have been considered unusual for David to want to show kindness to one of his descendants?

8. Why was it important to David to honor the promise that he made to Jonathan? What does this say about the importance of keeping the promises you make?

9. What were some of the challenges David faced in locating one of Saul's descendants? What does this say about the challenges you might face in keeping your promises?

10. What had happened to Mephibosheth—through no fault of his own? How do you relate the situation in which he found himself?

11. When have you experienced the kind of grace that David extended to Mephibosheth? How did you respond to that particular act of kindness?

12. How does David's story inspire you to show kindness to someone in your life this week?

LIFE LESSONS

We have much in common with Mephibosheth. We were born of royalty. We carry the wounds of a fall. We have lived in fear of a king we've never seen. We, like Mephibosheth, "were unable to help ourselves" (Romans 5:6 NCV). It took an act of mercy on David's part to find Mephibosheth, remove him from the land "without pasture" where he had been hiding, and invite him to sit at his table "like one of the king's sons" (2 Samuel 9:11). Likewise, it took an act of mercy on God's part to find us, remove us from our sinful situation (where we had been "hiding" from him), and invite us into his presence. But God did even more. As Paul would write, "The Spirit you received does not make you slaves, so that you live in fear again; rather, the Spirit you received brought about your adoption to sonship. And by him we cry, '*Abba*, Father'" (Romans 8:15).

DEVOTION

Lord, I praise you for seeking me while I was yet a sinner. I thank you for bringing me to your table and inviting me to join your family. Help me to never take this act of mercy for granted but to be one who shares the grace that you have extended to me with others.

JOURNALING

Have you made a promise to someone but failed to follow through on it? Ask the Holy Spirit to bring any such situation to mind and then write out what you will do to fulfill that promise.

FOR FURTHER READING

To complete the book of 2 Samuel during this twelve-part study, read 2 Samuel 9:1–10:19. For more Bible passages about honesty and integrity, read Numbers 30:1–2; Leviticus 19:11; Proverbs 11:3; Luke 16:10; 2 Corinthians 8:21; Colossians 3:9; Titus 2:7–8; 1 John 2:5.

LESSON SEVEN

COLOSSAL COLLAPSES

The woman was very beautiful, and David sent someone to find out about her.
2 Samuel 11:2–3

REFLECTION

What are some of the strategies you have witnessed the enemy use when it comes to temptation?

SITUATION

When David learned the king of the Ammonites had died—a man who had shown kindness to him in the past—he sent a delegation to Hanun, the new king, to express his condolences. However, Hanun's advisors, suspecting the envoys to be spies, humiliated David's men by shaving off half their beards and cutting their garments at the waist before sending them back. The Ammonites then hired twenty thousand Aramean foot soldiers, raised up thousands more, and went to war. David responded by sending out Joab and his army to confront the threat. Joab divided his forces, leading one group against the Arameans while his brother Abishai faced the Ammonites. The Arameans fled before Joab, and the Ammonites retreated when they saw their allies were defeated. The Arameans soon regrouped, but David personally led his forces to a decisive victory against them, killing seven hundred charioteers and forty thousand horsemen. The Arameans made peace with Israel, leaving the Ammonites isolated. David should have continued to lead his soldiers at this point, but instead he again sent out Joab to pursue his foes.

OBSERVATION

Read 2 Samuel 11:1–17 from the New International Version or the New King James Version.

NEW INTERNATIONAL VERSION

1 In the spring, at the time when kings go off to war, David sent Joab out
with the king's men and the whole Israelite army. They destroyed the
Ammonites and besieged Rabbah. But David remained in Jerusalem.

2 One evening David got up from his bed and walked around on the
roof of the palace. From the roof he saw a woman bathing. The woman
was very beautiful, 3 and David sent someone to find out about her. The
man said, "She is Bathsheba, the daughter of Eliam and the wife of Uriah
the Hittite." 4 Then David sent messengers to get her. She came to him,
and he slept with her. (Now she was purifying herself from her monthly
uncleanness.) Then she went back home. 5 The woman conceived and
sent word to David, saying, "I am pregnant."

6 So David sent this word to Joab: "Send me Uriah the Hittite." And
Joab sent him to David. 7 When Uriah came to him, David asked him
how Joab was, how the soldiers were and how the war was going. 8 Then
David said to Uriah, "Go down to your house and wash your feet." So
Uriah left the palace, and a gift from the king was sent after him. 9 But
Uriah slept at the entrance to the palace with all his master's servants and
did not go down to his house.

10 David was told, "Uriah did not go home." So he asked Uriah, "Haven't
you just come from a military campaign? Why didn't you go home?"

11 Uriah said to David, "The ark and Israel and Judah are staying in
tents, and my commander Joab and my lord's men are camped in the

open country. How could I go to my house to eat and drink and make
love to my wife? As surely as you live, I will not do such a thing!"
[12] Then David said to him, "Stay here one more day, and tomorrow
I will send you back." So Uriah remained in Jerusalem that day and the
next. [13] At David's invitation, he ate and drank with him, and David
made him drunk. But in the evening Uriah went out to sleep on his mat
among his master's servants; he did not go home.

[14] In the morning David wrote a letter to Joab and sent it with Uriah.
[15] In it he wrote, "Put Uriah out in front where the fighting is fiercest.
Then withdraw from him so he will be struck down and die."

[16] So while Joab had the city under siege, he put Uriah at a place
where he knew the strongest defenders were. [17] When the men of the city
came out and fought against Joab, some of the men in David's army fell;
moreover, Uriah the Hittite died.

New King James Version

[1] It happened in the spring of the year, at the time when kings go out to
battle, that David sent Joab and his servants with him, and all Israel; and
they destroyed the people of Ammon and besieged Rabbah. But David
remained at Jerusalem.

[2] Then it happened one evening that David arose from his bed and
walked on the roof of the king's house. And from the roof he saw a
woman bathing, and the woman was very beautiful to behold. [3] So David
sent and inquired about the woman. And someone said, "Is this not
Bathsheba, the daughter of Eliam, the wife of Uriah the Hittite?" [4] Then
David sent messengers, and took her; and she came to him, and he lay
with her, for she was cleansed from her impurity; and she returned to her
house. [5] And the woman conceived; so she sent and told David, and said,
"I am with child."

[6] Then David sent to Joab, saying, "Send me Uriah the Hittite." And
Joab sent Uriah to David. [7] When Uriah had come to him, David asked
how Joab was doing, and how the people were doing, and how the war
prospered. [8] And David said to Uriah, "Go down to your house and wash

your feet." So Uriah departed from the king's house, and a gift of food
from the king followed him. [9] But Uriah slept at the door of the king's
house with all the servants of his lord, and did not go down to his house.
[10] So when they told David, saying, "Uriah did not go down to his house,"
David said to Uriah, "Did you not come from a journey? Why did you
not go down to your house?"

[11] And Uriah said to David, "The ark and Israel and Judah are dwelling in tents, and my lord Joab and the servants of my lord are encamped
in the open fields. Shall I then go to my house to eat and drink, and to lie
with my wife? As you live, and as your soul lives, I will not do this thing."

[12] Then David said to Uriah, "Wait here today also, and tomorrow
I will let you depart." So Uriah remained in Jerusalem that day and the
next. [13] Now when David called him, he ate and drank before him; and he
made him drunk. And at evening he went out to lie on his bed with the
servants of his lord, but he did not go down to his house.

[14] In the morning it happened that David wrote a letter to Joab and
sent it by the hand of Uriah. [15] And he wrote in the letter, saying, "Set
Uriah in the forefront of the hottest battle, and retreat from him, that he
may be struck down and die." [16] So it was, while Joab besieged the city,
that he assigned Uriah to a place where he knew there were valiant men.
[17] Then the men of the city came out and fought with Joab. And some of
the people of the servants of David fell; and Uriah the Hittite died also.

EXPLORATION

1. David had just led his army in a major battle against the Arameans. How might this have led to him *not* personally leading his army against the Ammonite threat?

2. How do you think David's decision to remain in Jerusalem might have opened him up to temptation?

3. What did the messenger report about Bathsheba? What is the significance of him saying she was "the wife of Uriah" (2 Samuel 11:3)?

4. What was King David's first plan when he learned that Bathsheba was pregnant?

5. Why did Uriah choose to sleep at the entrance of the palace instead of going home?

6. What was David's final plan to get rid of Uriah in order to cover up the sin he had committed?

INSPIRATION

It's springtime in Israel. The nights are warm, and the air is sweet. David has time on his hands, love on his mind, and people at his disposal.

His eyes fall upon a woman as she bathes. We'll always wonder if Bathsheba was bathing in a place where she shouldn't bathe, hoping David would look where he shouldn't look. We'll never know. But we know that he looks and likes what he sees. So he inquires about her. A servant returns with this information: "She is Bathsheba, the daughter of Eliam and the wife of Uriah the Hittite" (2 Samuel 11:3).

The servant laces his information with a warning. He gives not only the woman's name but her marital status and the name of her husband. Why tell David she is married if not to caution him? And why give the husband's name unless David is familiar with it?

Odds are, David knew Uriah. The servant hopes to deftly dissuade the king. But David misses the hint. The next verse describes his first step down a greasy slope. "Then David sent messengers to get her. She came to him, and he slept with her" (verse 4).

David "sends" many times in this story. He sends Joab to battle (see verse 1). He sends the servant to inquire about Bathsheba and then sends for Bathsheba to have her come to him (see verses 3–4). When David learns of her pregnancy, he sends word to Joab (see verse 6) to send Uriah back to Jerusalem. David sends him to Bathsheba to rest, but Uriah is too noble. David opts to send Uriah back to a place in the battle where he is sure to be killed. Thinking his cover-up is complete, David sends for Bathsheba and marries her (see verse 27).

We don't like this sending, demanding David. We much prefer the pastoring David, caring for the flock; the dashing David, hiding from Saul; the worshiping David, penning psalms. We aren't prepared for the David who has lost control of his self-control, who sins as he sends.

The story of David and Bathsheba is less a story of lust and more a story of power. A story of a man who rose too high for his own good.

A man who needed to hear these words: "Come down before you fall." (From *Facing Your Giants* by Max Lucado.)

REACTION

7. Read 1 Corinthians 10:12. What warning does Paul give in this verse to those who—like David—believe they are secure and "standing firm"?

8. When is a time that you—like King David—ignored a caution and later regretted it? What led you to dismiss that particular warning?

9. When is a time that you were tempted to justify a wrong decision that you made? What did you ultimately end up doing in that situation?

10. Read James 5:16. Who in your life helps you to be accountable before God? What is the value of having such an accountability partner?

11. What do you learn from this story about wielding any power you have over others wisely?

12. What do you learn in this story about the dangers of pride?

LIFE LESSONS

Sin has a habit of breeding more sin. David sinned when he committed adultery with Bathsheba. He should have confessed this sin and dealt with the consequences of his actions. But instead, he attempted to cover up what he had done. David did everything he could to convince Uriah to return home and sleep with his wife. He wanted to deceive Uriah into believing the child whom she would soon bear was his own. When this plot failed, David arranged for Uriah to be killed in battle, compounding one dire sin upon another. In this way, he demonstrated the truth of what James would later write: "After desire has conceived, it gives birth to sin; and sin, when it is full-grown, gives birth to death" (James 1:15).

DEVOTION

Heavenly Father, I confess that I often allow pride to gain a foothold in my life. I ask for you to search my heart and bring to light anything I am holding on to that is not pleasing to you. Help me to stay humble before you and always be willing to confess my sins when I fall.

JOURNALING

What practical steps do you take to remain humble before God so that you don't fall into pride? Take a few moments to write down your thoughts in the space below.

FOR FURTHER READING

To complete the book of 2 Samuel during this twelve-part study, read 2 Samuel 11:1–27. For more Bible passages about resisting temptation, read Genesis 3:1; Exodus 34:12; Psalm 119:110; Matthew 4:10–11; 1 Corinthians 10:13; Colossians 3:5; 2 Timothy 2:22; James 1:13.

LESSON EIGHT

A SENTENCE LEVIED

"Now, therefore, the sword will never depart from your house, because you despised me and took the wife of Uriah the Hittite to be your own."

2 Samuel 12:10

REFLECTION

What is the danger in thinking you can hide your sin from the Lord?

SITUATION

David, in his two decades on the throne, had distinguished himself as a warrior, musician, statesman, and king. His cabinet was strong, his kingdom was expanding, his battle record was impressive, and he was beloved by the people. David was never higher, but also never weaker, which led to him committing adultery with Bathsheba. When she was found to be with child, he ordered her husband, Uriah, to be sent into the front lines of the battle against the Ammonites. This order was carried out by Joab, who reported back to David that Uriah had indeed been killed. Following this, Bathsheba mourned for her husband, and then she became another of David's many wives. The king thought he had literally gotten away with murder. However, God was about to intervene to let David know that he knew all about his sinful actions.

OBSERVATION

Read 2 Samuel 12:1–14 from the New International Version or the New King James Version.

NEW INTERNATIONAL VERSION

1 The LORD sent Nathan to David. When he came to him, he said, "There
were two men in a certain town, one rich and the other poor. 2 The rich
man had a very large number of sheep and cattle, 3 but the poor man
had nothing except one little ewe lamb he had bought. He raised it, and
it grew up with him and his children. It shared his food, drank from his
cup and even slept in his arms. It was like a daughter to him.
4 "Now a traveler came to the rich man, but the rich man refrained
from taking one of his own sheep or cattle to prepare a meal for the traveler who had come to him. Instead, he took the ewe lamb that belonged
to the poor man and prepared it for the one who had come to him."
5 David burned with anger against the man and said to Nathan,
"As surely as the LORD lives, the man who did this must die! 6 He must
pay for that lamb four times over, because he did such a thing and had
no pity."
7 Then Nathan said to David, "You are the man! This is what the
LORD, the God of Israel, says: 'I anointed you king over Israel, and I
delivered you from the hand of Saul. 8 I gave your master's house to you,
and your master's wives into your arms. I gave you all Israel and Judah.
And if all this had been too little, I would have given you even more. 9
Why did you despise the word of the LORD by doing what is evil in his
eyes? You struck down Uriah the Hittite with the sword and took his
wife to be your own. You killed him with the sword of the Ammonites.
10 Now, therefore, the sword will never depart from your house, because
you despised me and took the wife of Uriah the Hittite to be your own.'
11 "This is what the LORD says: 'Out of your own household I am
going to bring calamity on you. Before your very eyes I will take your
wives and give them to one who is close to you, and he will sleep with

your wives in broad daylight. 12 You did it in secret, but I will do this
thing in broad daylight before all Israel.'"

13 Then David said to Nathan, "I have sinned against the LORD."

Nathan replied, "The LORD has taken away your sin. You are not
going to die. 14 But because by doing this you have shown utter contempt
for the LORD, the son born to you will die."

NEW KING JAMES VERSION

1 Then the LORD sent Nathan to David. And he came to him, and said
to him: "There were two men in one city, one rich and the other poor.
2 The rich man had exceedingly many flocks and herds. 3 But the poor
man had nothing, except one little ewe lamb which he had bought and
nourished; and it grew up together with him and with his children. It ate
of his own food and drank from his own cup and lay in his bosom; and
it was like a daughter to him. 4 And a traveler came to the rich man, who
refused to take from his own flock and from his own herd to prepare one
for the wayfaring man who had come to him; but he took the poor man's
lamb and prepared it for the man who had come to him."

5 So David's anger was greatly aroused against the man, and he said
to Nathan, "As the LORD lives, the man who has done this shall surely
die! 6 And he shall restore fourfold for the lamb, because he did this thing
and because he had no pity."

7 Then Nathan said to David, "You are the man! Thus says the LORD
God of Israel: 'I anointed you king over Israel, and I delivered you from
the hand of Saul. 8 I gave you your master's house and your master's
wives into your keeping, and gave you the house of Israel and Judah.
And if that had been too little, I also would have given you much more! 9
Why have you despised the commandment of the LORD, to do evil in His
sight? You have killed Uriah the Hittite with the sword; you have taken
his wife to be your wife, and have killed him with the sword of the people
of Ammon. 10 Now therefore, the sword shall never depart from your
house, because you have despised Me, and have taken the wife of Uriah
the Hittite to be your wife.' 11 Thus says the LORD: 'Behold, I will raise up

adversity against you from your own house; and I will take your wives before your eyes and give them to your neighbor, and he shall lie with your wives in the sight of this sun. [12] For you did it secretly, but I will do this thing before all Israel, before the sun.'"

[13] So David said to Nathan, "I have sinned against the LORD."

And Nathan said to David, "The LORD also has put away your sin; you shall not die. [14] However, because by this deed you have given great occasion to the enemies of the LORD to blaspheme, the child also who is born to you shall surely die."

EXPLORATION

1. Review 2 Samuel 11:27. This is the only time God is mentioned in this entire chapter. What might this indicate about David's state of mind at this point in his reign?

2. What approach did Nathan take to confront David about his sin?

3. How did David react when Nathan told him the story about the rich man taking the one lamb that the poor man owned—which he cherished?

4. In what ways had David acted like the rich man in Nathan's story?

5. What did the Lord say would happen to David and his household because of his sin?

6. How did David respond when his sin was exposed in this way?

INSPIRATION

Underline the last verse of 2 Samuel chapter 11: "The thing David had done displeased the LORD" (verse 27). With these words, the narrator introduces a new character into the David and Bathsheba drama: God. Thus far, he's been absent from the text, unmentioned in the story.

God will be silent no more. The name is not mentioned until the final verse of chapter 11 dominates chapter 12. David, the "sender," sits while God takes control.

God sends Nathan to David. Nathan is a prophet, a preacher, a White House chaplain of sorts. The man deserves a medal for going to the king. He knows what happened to Uriah. David had killed an innocent soldier. What will he do with a confronting preacher?

Still, Nathan goes. Rather than declare the deed, he relates a story about a poor man with one sheep. David instantly connects. Nathan tells him how the poor shepherd loved this sheep—holding her in his own lap, feeding her from his own plate. She was all he had.

Enter the rich jerk. A traveler stops by his mansion, so a feast is in order. Rather than slaughter a sheep from his own flock, the rich man sends his bodyguards to steal the poor man's animal. They Hummer onto his property, snatch the lamb, and fire up the barbecue.

As David listens, hair rises on his neck. He grips the arms of the throne. He renders a verdict without a trial: fish bait by nightfall. "As surely as the LORD lives, the man who did this must die! He must pay for that lamb four times over, because he did such a thing and had no pity" (12:5–6). Oh, David. You never saw it coming, did you? You never saw Nathan erecting the gallows or throwing the rope over the beam.

"Then Nathan said to David, 'You are the man!'" (verse 7).

David's face pales. His Adam's apple bounces. A bead of sweat forms on his forehead. He slinks back in his chair. He makes no defense. He utters no response. He has nothing to say. God, however, is just clearing his throat. Through Nathan he proclaims, "Why have you treated the word of GOD with brazen contempt, doing this great evil? You murdered Uriah the Hittite, then took his wife as your wife" (verse 9 MSG).

God's words reflect hurt, not hate. Your flock fills the hills. Why rob? Beauty populates your palace. Why take from someone else? Why would the wealthy steal? David has no excuse.

So God levies a sentence. "Now, therefore, the sword will never depart from your house, because you despised me and took the wife of Uriah the Hittite to be your own. . . . You did it in secret, but I will do this thing in broad daylight before all Israel" (verses 10, 12).

From this day forward, turmoil and tragedy mark David's family. Surrounding nations now question the holiness of David's God. David had soiled God's reputation, blemished God's honor. And God, who jealously guards his glory, punishes David's public sin in a public fashion. The infant perishes. And the king of Israel discovers the harsh truth of Numbers 32:23: "You may be sure that your sin will find you out." (From *Facing Your Giants* by Max Lucado.)

REACTION

7. Nine months (at least) had passed between David's sin and the prophet Nathan's conviction. Why do you think David chose not to confess his sin during all that time?

8. What did it require on Nathan's part to confront King David? When has God called you to do something similar for a friend or loved one?

9. What tactic did Nathan use to help David realize the depth of his sin? When has God used a similar tactic to help you recognize the harm your sin caused?

10. How do you tend to respond when you are confronted with your own wrongdoing?

11. Read Matthew 7:3–5. What does Jesus say about the importance of recognizing *your* faults before addressing the faults of others?

12. When you consider David's story, why is it so important to make sure your actions reflect integrity—even when no one else is watching?

LIFE LESSONS

"Against you, you only, have I sinned" (Psalm 51:4). David wrote these words after Nathan *confronted* him with his sin. If David had adopted this perspective after *committing* his sin, he would have been quick to repent—and avoided the tragedy that followed. David was concerned about his reputation as king and what the people would think. God, meanwhile, was concerned about his relationship with David. Today, the world tells us that we must protect our reputation at all costs and keep up appearances. God, however, tells us that we must protect our relationship with him. He wants his people to recognize that every sin puts distance between himself and us. "But your iniquities have separated you from your God; your sins have hidden his face from you" (Isaiah 59:2).

DEVOTION

God, I want to have the perspective that my sin keeps me from growing in my relationship with you. I pray that my heart will not grow calloused to your promptings and convictions. Lead me to confess my sins when I commit them and to never try and hide my deeds from you.

JOURNALING

Read all of David's confession in Psalm 51. In the space below, write out your own confession for any sins that you have not yet brought before God—and then ask for his forgiveness.

FOR FURTHER READING

To complete the book of 2 Samuel during this twelve-part study, read 2 Samuel 12:1–14:33. For more Bible passages about confession and repentance, read Proverbs 28:13; Ezekiel 18:32; Zechariah 1:3; Matthew 4:17; Luke 15:7; Acts 3:19; 2 Peter 3:9; Revelation 2:5.

LESSON NINE

FAMILY BETRAYALS

Then David said to all his officials who were with him in Jerusalem, "Come! We must flee, or none of us will escape from Absalom."
2 Samuel 15:14

REFLECTION

How would you describe your relationship with your immediate family? What are some of the challenges you face?

SITUATION

Nathan's prophecy concerning the child born to David and Bathsheba came true when the infant fell gravely ill and died after seven days. David, who had been fasting and praying for the child's recovery, ended his time of mourning, worshiped the Lord, and comforted Bathsheba. Later, she gave birth to their second child, whom they named Solomon. Meanwhile, David's son Amnon deceived and raped his half-sister Tamar. Absalom, her brother, was enraged by the act and plotted for two years before killing Amnon at a feast. Fearing David's wrath, Absalom fled to Geshur, where he lived in exile for three years. David mourned for Amnon yet longed to be reconciled with Absalom. So Joab orchestrated Absalom's return to Jerusalem—though the king refused to see him for two years. Eventually, with Joab's help, Absalom was allowed back into David's presence, and the two reconciled. However, this would not be the end of their story, for Absalom began to ingratiate himself with the people and conspire to take the throne.

OBSERVATION

Read 2 Samuel 15:1–18 from the New International Version or the New King James Version.

New International Version

1 In the course of time, Absalom provided himself with a chariot and
horses and with fifty men to run ahead of him. 2 He would get up early
and stand by the side of the road leading to the city gate. Whenever anyone came with a complaint to be placed before the king for a decision,
Absalom would call out to him, "What town are you from?" He would
answer, "Your servant is from one of the tribes of Israel." 3 Then Absalom
would say to him, "Look, your claims are valid and proper, but there is no
representative of the king to hear you." 4 And Absalom would add, "If only
I were appointed judge in the land! Then everyone who has a complaint
or case could come to me and I would see that they receive justice."

5 Also, whenever anyone approached him to bow down before him,
Absalom would reach out his hand, take hold of him and kiss him. 6
Absalom behaved in this way toward all the Israelites who came to the
king asking for justice, and so he stole the hearts of the people of Israel.

7 At the end of four years, Absalom said to the king, "Let me go to
Hebron and fulfill a vow I made to the Lord. 8 While your servant was
living at Geshur in Aram, I made this vow: 'If the Lord takes me back to
Jerusalem, I will worship the Lord in Hebron.'"

9 The king said to him, "Go in peace." So he went to Hebron.

10 Then Absalom sent secret messengers throughout the tribes of Israel to say, "As soon as you hear the sound of the trumpets, then say, 'Absalom is king in Hebron.'" 11 Two hundred men from Jerusalem had accompanied Absalom. They had been invited as guests and went quite innocently, knowing nothing about the matter. 12 While Absalom was offering sacrifices, he also sent for Ahithophel the Gilonite, David's counselor, to come from Giloh, his hometown. And so the conspiracy gained strength, and Absalom's following kept on increasing.

13 A messenger came and told David, "The hearts of the people of Israel are with Absalom."

14 Then David said to all his officials who were with him in Jerusalem, "Come! We must flee, or none of us will escape from Absalom. We must leave immediately, or he will move quickly to overtake us and bring ruin on us and put the city to the sword."

15 The king's officials answered him, "Your servants are ready to do whatever our lord the king chooses."

16 The king set out, with his entire household following him; but he left ten concubines to take care of the palace. 17 So the king set out, with all the people following him, and they halted at the edge of the city. 18 All his men marched past him, along with all the Kerethites and Pelethites; and all the six hundred Gittites who had accompanied him from Gath marched before the king.

New King James Version

1 After this it happened that Absalom provided himself with chariots and horses, and fifty men to run before him. 2 Now Absalom would rise early and stand beside the way to the gate. So it was, whenever anyone who had a lawsuit came to the king for a decision, that Absalom would call to him and say, "What city are you from?" And he would say, "Your servant is from such and such a tribe of Israel." 3 Then Absalom would say to him, "Look, your case is good and right; but there is no deputy of the king to hear you." 4 Moreover Absalom would say, "Oh, that I were

made judge in the land, and everyone who has any suit or cause would
come to me; then I would give him justice." 5 And so it was, whenever
anyone came near to bow down to him, that he would put out his hand
and take him and kiss him. 6 In this manner Absalom acted toward all
Israel who came to the king for judgment. So Absalom stole the hearts
of the men of Israel.

7 Now it came to pass after forty years that Absalom said to the king,
"Please, let me go to Hebron and pay the vow which I made to the LORD. 8
For your servant took a vow while I dwelt at Geshur in Syria, saying, 'If the
LORD indeed brings me back to Jerusalem, then I will serve the LORD.'"

9 And the king said to him, "Go in peace." So he arose and went to
Hebron.

10 Then Absalom sent spies throughout all the tribes of Israel, saying, "As soon as you hear the sound of the trumpet, then you shall say,
'Absalom reigns in Hebron!'" 11 And with Absalom went two hundred
men invited from Jerusalem, and they went along innocently and did
not know anything. 12 Then Absalom sent for Ahithophel the Gilonite,
David's counselor, from his city—from Giloh—while he offered sacrifices. And the conspiracy grew strong, for the people with Absalom
continually increased in number.

13 Now a messenger came to David, saying, "The hearts of the men of
Israel are with Absalom."

14 So David said to all his servants who were with him at Jerusalem,
"Arise, and let us flee, or we shall not escape from Absalom. Make haste
to depart, lest he overtake us suddenly and bring disaster upon us, and
strike the city with the edge of the sword."

15 And the king's servants said to the king, "We are your servants,
ready to do whatever my lord the king commands." 16 Then the king went
out with all his household after him. But the king left ten women, concubines, to keep the house. 17 And the king went out with all the people after
him, and stopped at the outskirts. 18 Then all his servants passed before
him; and all the Cherethites, all the Pelethites, and all the Gittites, six
hundred men who had followed him from Gath, passed before the king.

EXPLORATION

1. Review 2 Samuel 13:21 and 39. What did David fail to do when he learned of Amnon's horrible deed? What did he fail to do when Absalom then killed Amnon?

2. What was the significance of Absalom providing himself with a chariot and having fifty men run ahead of him? What was Absalom portraying to the people?

3. How did Absalom's actions at the city gate help him gain the loyalty of the Israelites?

4. What does Absalom's statement, "If only I were appointed judge in the land" (1 Samuel 15:4), reveal about his ambitions and intentions?

5. How did Absalom's conspiracy gain strength over time? What role did Ahithophel play in it?

6. What was David's response when he learned the people were supporting Absalom as king?

INSPIRATION

David looks older than his sixty-plus years. His shoulders slump; his head hangs. This is the longest path he's ever walked. Longer than the winding road from fugitive to king or the guilty road from conviction to confession. Those trails bore some steep turns. But none compare with the ascent up the Mount of Olives. "But David continued up the Mount of Olives, weeping as he went; his head was covered and he was barefoot" (2 Samuel 15:30).

Look carefully and you'll find the cause of David's tears. He wears no crown. His son Absalom has taken it by force. David has no home. Those walls rising to his back belong to the city of Jerusalem. He flees the capital he founded. Who wouldn't weep at a time like this? No throne. No home. Jerusalem behind him and the wilderness ahead of him.

Thirteen years have passed since Nathan told David, "The sword will never depart from your house" (12:10). Nathan's prophecy has proved painfully true. One of David's sons, Amnon, fell in lust with his half-sister Tamar, one of David's daughters by another marriage. Amnon pined, plotted, and raped her. After the rape, he discarded Tamar like a worn doll.

Tamar, understandably, came undone. She threw ashes on her head and tore the robe of many colors worn by virgin daughters of the king. She "remained desolate in her brother Absalom's house" (13:20 NKJV). The next verse tells us David's response: "But when King David heard of all these things, he was very angry" (verse 21 NKJV).

That's it? That's all? We want a few verbs. *Confront* will do. *Punish* would be nice. *Banish* even better. But what did David do to Amnon? *Nothing.* No lecture. No penalty. No imprisonment. No dressing down. No chewing out.

Even worse, he did nothing for Tamar. She needed his protection, his affirmation and validation. She needed a dad. What she got was silence. So Absalom, her brother, filled the void. He sheltered his sister, got Amnon drunk, and had him killed.

David had eight spouses. He fathered other children through concubines. And he neglected all the children he had with them. Going AWOL on his family was David's greatest failure. Seducing Bathsheba was an inexcusable but explicable act of passion. Murdering Uriah was a ruthless yet predictable deed from a desperate heart. But passive parenting and widespread philandering? These were not sins of a slothful afternoon or the deranged reactions of self-defense. David's family foul-up was a lifelong stupor that cost him dearly.

Absalom ultimately resolved to overthrow his father. He recruited from David's army and staged a coup. Loyalists of David eventually chased him down. When the would-be ruler tried to escape on horseback, his long hair got tangled in a tree, and soldiers speared him. David heard the news and fell to pieces: "O my son Absalom—my son, my son Absalom—if only I had died in your place! O Absalom my son, my son!" (18:33 NKJV). Tardy tears.

How do we explain David's disastrous home? Was he too busy to notice them? Maybe. He had a city to settle and a kingdom to build.

Was he too important to care for them? Perhaps. Was he too guilty to shepherd them? Quite possibly. After all, how could David, who had seduced Bathsheba and murdered Uriah, correct his sons when they raped and murdered?

Too busy. Too important. Too guilty. And now? Too late. A dozen exits too late. But it's not too late for you. Your home is your giant-size privilege, your towering priority. So do not make David's tragic mistake. (From *Facing Your Giants* by Max Lucado.)

REACTION

7. What steps do you take to ensure you are prioritizing your family in the midst of all the demands that are made on your time?

8. When have you avoided addressing a difficult situation in your family? When you look back, what might have been the consequences of your inaction?

9. What does David's story reveal about the importance of showing support to loved ones and being present with them in painful times?

10. Read Proverbs 22:6 and Ephesians 6:4. What responsibilities do parents have when it comes to training and disciplining their children?

11. What role might guilt have played in David's decision not to correct his sons? How do you handle feelings of guilt when it comes to your family relationships?

12. What legacy do you want to leave for your family? How are you building that legacy?

LIFE LESSONS

Absalom was a man with great charisma. He was "praised for his handsome appearance" (2 Samuel 14:25) and had such a magnetic personality that he "stole the hearts of the people" (15:6). He also had the best pedigree in the land. His father was a king and his mother, Maakah, was the daughter of a king (see 3:3). Absalom had the potential to become a great leader—but he threw it all away when he sought to lift himself up. Absalom's attitude is prevalent in the world today. We are taught that if we don't lift ourselves up, nobody else will. However, God teaches us that if we humble ourselves before him, *he* will lift us up (see James 4:10).

DEVOTION

Lord, I don't want to run from your discipline. I welcome your correction, as I know it will keep me in right standing before you. I humble myself before you and ask that you lift me up. Thank you for being a Father who loves me enough to not allow me to keep on sinning.

JOURNALING

Think about the relationship you had with a parent or other caregiver growing up. What are a few things you can name that you are glad that person taught you?

FOR FURTHER READING

To complete the book of 2 Samuel during this twelve-part study, read 2 Samuel 15:1–17:29. For more Bible passages about God's discipline, read Job 5:17; Proverbs 3:11–12; 10:17; Psalm 94:12; 1 Corinthians 9:27; Titus 1:8; Hebrews 12:5–6.

LESSON 10

THE RETURN OF THE KING

He won over the hearts of the men of Judah so that they were all of one mind. They sent word to the king, "Return, you and all your men."
2 Samuel 19:14

REFLECTION

What makes it the most difficult for you to forgive those who have wronged you?

SITUATION

David had been forced to flee Jerusalem after Absalom successfully won the hearts and minds of the people. Fortunately, a few loyal followers joined him in this flight, including a man named Hushai, whom David sent back to serve as a spy and counter to Absalom's advisor. David continued his flight and was met by a man named Shimei, a relative of Saul, who cursed David and pelted his men with stones. Meanwhile, back in Jerusalem, Hushai successfully persuaded Absalom to delay an attack against David. This gave David's forces time to regroup and engage Absalom's army in the forest of Ephraim. David had given orders for Absalom to be spared, but when Joab found him caught in a tree by his hair, he plunged three javelins into his heart. David was overcome with grief when he learned of Absalom's death, but eventually he heeded Joab's advice not to prioritize his sorrow over the morale of his troops. Now, with Absalom's rebellion finally put down, David had to decide what to do with those who had betrayed him.

OBSERVATION

Read 2 Samuel 19:9–23 from the New International Version or the New King James Version.

New International Version

9 Throughout the tribes of Israel, all the people were arguing among
themselves, saying, "The king delivered us from the hand of our enemies; he is the one who rescued us from the hand of the Philistines. But
now he has fled the country to escape from Absalom; 10 and Absalom,
whom we anointed to rule over us, has died in battle. So why do you say
nothing about bringing the king back?"

11 King David sent this message to Zadok and Abiathar, the priests:
"Ask the elders of Judah, 'Why should you be the last to bring the king
back to his palace, since what is being said throughout Israel has reached
the king at his quarters? 12 You are my relatives, my own flesh and blood.
So why should you be the last to bring back the king?' 13 And say to
Amasa, 'Are you not my own flesh and blood? May God deal with me,
be it ever so severely, if you are not the commander of my army for life
in place of Joab.'"

14 He won over the hearts of the men of Judah so that they were all of
one mind. They sent word to the king, "Return, you and all your men."
15 Then the king returned and went as far as the Jordan.

Now the men of Judah had come to Gilgal to go out and meet the king
and bring him across the Jordan. 16 Shimei son of Gera, the Benjamite
from Bahurim, hurried down with the men of Judah to meet King David.

[17] With him were a thousand Benjamites, along with Ziba, the steward of Saul's household, and his fifteen sons and twenty servants. They rushed to the Jordan, where the king was. [18] They crossed at the ford to take the king's household over and to do whatever he wished.

When Shimei son of Gera crossed the Jordan, he fell prostrate before the king [19] and said to him, "May my lord not hold me guilty. Do not remember how your servant did wrong on the day my lord the king left Jerusalem. May the king put it out of his mind. [20] For I your servant know that I have sinned, but today I have come here as the first from the tribes of Joseph to come down and meet my lord the king."

[21] Then Abishai son of Zeruiah said, "Shouldn't Shimei be put to death for this? He cursed the LORD's anointed."

[22] David replied, "What does this have to do with you, you sons of Zeruiah? What right do you have to interfere? Should anyone be put to death in Israel today? Don't I know that today I am king over Israel?" [23] So the king said to Shimei, "You shall not die." And the king promised him on oath.

New King James Version

[9] Now all the people were in a dispute throughout all the tribes of Israel, saying, "The king saved us from the hand of our enemies, he delivered us from the hand of the Philistines, and now he has fled from the land because of Absalom. [10] But Absalom, whom we anointed over us, has died in battle. Now therefore, why do you say nothing about bringing back the king?"

[11] So King David sent to Zadok and Abiathar the priests, saying, "Speak to the elders of Judah, saying, 'Why are you the last to bring the king back to his house, since the words of all Israel have come to the king, to his very house? [12] You are my brethren, you are my bone and my flesh. Why then are you the last to bring back the king?' [13] And say to Amasa, 'Are you not my bone and my flesh? God do so to me, and more also, if you are not commander of the army before me continually in place of Joab.'" [14] So he swayed the hearts of all the men of Judah, just as the heart

of one man, so that they sent this word to the king: "Return, you and all
your servants!"

[15] Then the king returned and came to the Jordan. And Judah came
to Gilgal, to go to meet the king, to escort the king across the Jordan.
[16] And Shimei the son of Gera, a Benjamite, who was from Bahurim, hurried and came down with the men of Judah to meet King David. [17] There
were a thousand men of Benjamin with him, and Ziba the servant of the
house of Saul, and his fifteen sons and his twenty servants with him; and
they went over the Jordan before the king. [18] Then a ferryboat went across
to carry over the king's household, and to do what he thought good.

Now Shimei the son of Gera fell down before the king when he
had crossed the Jordan. [19] Then he said to the king, "Do not let my lord
impute iniquity to me, or remember what wrong your servant did on the
day that my lord the king left Jerusalem, that the king should take it to
heart. [20] For I, your servant, know that I have sinned. Therefore here I am,
the first to come today of all the house of Joseph to go down to meet my
lord the king."

[21] But Abishai the son of Zeruiah answered and said, "Shall not
Shimei be put to death for this, because he cursed the LORD's anointed?"

[22] And David said, "What have I to do with you, you sons of Zeruiah,
that you should be adversaries to me today? Shall any man be put to
death today in Israel? For do I not know that today I am king over Israel?"
[23] Therefore the king said to Shimei, "You shall not die." And the king
swore to him.

EXPLORATION

1. What arguments were the tribes of Israel having over David? What reasons did some have for wanting to restore David to the throne?

2. What appeal did David make to the elders of Judah as to why they should bring him back to the throne?

3. Review 2 Samuel 17:25 and 18:10–15. Who was Amasa? What might have motivated David to promise to make him the commander of his army in place of Joab?

4. Now look at 2 Samuel 16:5–10. What did Shimei do as David was fleeing Jerusalem? How did Abishai, a military commander, react when Shimei did these things?

5. What did Shimei do when he learned that David was returning to Jerusalem? How did Abishai react when he saw Shimei do these things?

6. What does David's decision to spare Shimei's life reveal about his character and leadership?

INSPIRATION

David had been forced to flee the city of Jerusalem. Some of the people had remained loyal to him. But many had not. Notable among this group was a man named Shimei, who "pelted David and all the king's officials with stones." Shimei even cursed David and said, "Get out, get out, you murderer, you scoundrel!" (2 Samuel 16:6–7).

When David returned to power, he had a choice in how to deal with Shimei and the others who had opposed him. He could have ordered mass executions in retaliation, as many of the monarchs of his day had done. Instead, we find David extending mercy. "So the king said to Shimei, 'You shall not die.' And the king promised him on oath" (19:23).

What enabled David to do this? Perhaps he understood an important principle: *The grace-given give grace.* Forgiven people forgive people. The mercy-marinated drip mercy. "God is kind to you so you will change your hearts and lives" (Romans 2:4 NCV). The forgiven who won't forgive can expect a sad fate—a life full of many bad and bitter days. Hoard hurts in your heart and expect the joy level of a Siberian death camp.

A friend once shared with me the fate of a hoarding grandmother who refused to part with anything. Her family witnessed two terrible consequences: She lost sleep and treasures. She couldn't rest because junk covered her bed. She lost treasures because they were obscured by mountains of trash. Jewelry, photographs, favorite books—all were hidden.

No rest. No treasures. Squirrel away your hurts and expect the same. Or clean your house and give the day a fresh chance!

"But, Max, the hurt is so deep." I know. They took much. But why let them keep taking from you? Haven't they stolen enough? Refusing to forgive keeps them loitering, taking still.

"But, Max, what they did was so bad." You bet it was. Forgiveness does not mean approval. David certainly didn't say he approved of what Shimei and the others had done to him. You aren't endorsing misbehavior. Rather, you are choosing to entrust your offenders to "Him who judges righteously" (1 Peter 2:23 NKJV).

"But, Max, I've been so angry for so long." And forgiveness won't come overnight. But you can take baby steps in the direction of grace. Forgive in phases. Quit cussing the perpetrators. Start praying for them instead. Try to understand their situation.

In the end, we all choose what lives inside us. May you choose forgiveness. (From *Great Day Every Day* by Max Lucado.)

REACTION

7. Do you have a Shimei in your life—a person who likes to criticize you when you are down? How do you tend to deal with such a person?

8. David could have exacted revenge against those who had defected to Absalom's side. What do you think compelled him to show mercy?

9. Read Deuteronomy 32:35. What does this verse say about taking vengeance against others?

10. Look again at Romans 2:4. What do you need to remember when you are tempted to hold on to bitterness and not forgive others?

11. Are there any hurts that you have chosen to "squirrel away"? If so, what damage might this be inflicting on your heart and mind?

12. Forgiveness won't always come overnight. What "baby steps" can you take this week to at least *slightly* move in the direction of grace?

LIFE LESSONS

It would have been easy for David to exact revenge on Shimei and the others who had turned against him. He could have acted like Joab, who murdered Abner to avenge the blood of his brother Asahel (see 2 Samuel 3:27). He could have taken a page out of Absalom's book, who killed his half-brother Amnon to avenge Tamar (see 13:32). But instead, when David returned to Jerusalem as king, he declared, "Should anyone be put to death in Israel today?" (19:22). In extending mercy, David was demonstrating a principle later taught by Jesus: "Do not condemn, and you will not be condemned. Forgive, and you will be forgiven. . . . For with the measure you use, it will be measured to you" (Luke 6:37–38).

DEVOTION

Heavenly Father, it is so easy for me to become bitter. People do wrong to me . . . and my first instinct is to make them pay! I need your guidance and intervention when times get heated and I just want to lash out. Help me to forgive others as you have forgiven me.

JOURNALING

It can be easier to forgive others when you remember how God has forgiven you. Take a few minutes to write out some of the ways that God has forgiven your past mistakes.

FOR FURTHER READING

To complete the book of 2 Samuel during this twelve-part study, read 2 Samuel 18:1–20:26. For more Bible passages about letting go of vengeance and forgiving others, read Leviticus 19:18; Deuteronomy 32:35; Proverbs 20:22; Mark 11:25; Romans 12:19; Ephesians 4:32; 1 Thessalonians 5:15; 1 Peter 3:9.

LESSON 11

TAKING DOWN GIANTS

These four were descendants of Rapha in Gath, and they fell at the hands of David and his men.

2 Samuel 21:22

REFLECTION

What are the "giants" you still need to overcome with God's help?

SITUATION

David, after sparing Shimei's life, continued to navigate the aftermath of Absalom's rebellion. At one point he was met by Mephibosheth, the son of Jonathan, who claimed his servant Ziba had deceived him and slandered his good name. David, unsure of the truth, decided to divide Saul's land between the two men. Meanwhile, tensions arose between Judah and the other tribes over their roles in restoring David as king. The discord led to a rebellion by a man named Sheba, who marshalled his forces in the city of Abel Beth Maakah. When Joab arrived and began to besiege the city, the residents killed Sheba and threw his head down from the wall. The final four chapters of 2 Samuel form an epilogue to the book and depict other events that occurred during David's reign. In one story, a famine struck Israel, which David learned was due to Saul's unatoned bloodshed against the Gibeonites. David made amends by handing over seven of Saul's descendants to the Gibeonites to be executed. David then retrieved and properly buried the remains of Saul and Jonathan, as well as the men who had been executed.

OBSERVATION

Read 2 Samuel 21:15–22 from the New International Version or the New King James Version.

New International Version

15 Once again there was a battle between the Philistines and Israel. David
went down with his men to fight against the Philistines, and he became
exhausted. 16 And Ishbi-Benob, one of the descendants of Rapha, whose
bronze spearhead weighed three hundred shekels and who was armed
with a new sword, said he would kill David. 17 But Abishai son of Zeruiah
came to David's rescue; he struck the Philistine down and killed him.
Then David's men swore to him, saying, "Never again will you go out
with us to battle, so that the lamp of Israel will not be extinguished."

18 In the course of time, there was another battle with the Philistines,
at Gob. At that time Sibbekai the Hushathite killed Saph, one of the
descendants of Rapha.

19 In another battle with the Philistines at Gob, Elhanan son of Jair
the Bethlehemite killed the brother of Goliath the Gittite, who had a
spear with a shaft like a weaver's rod.

20 In still another battle, which took place at Gath, there was a huge
man with six fingers on each hand and six toes on each foot—twenty-four in all. He also was descended from Rapha. 21 When he taunted
Israel, Jonathan son of Shimeah, David's brother, killed him.

22 These four were descendants of Rapha in Gath, and they fell at the
hands of David and his men.

New King James Version

15 When the Philistines were at war again with Israel, David and his servants with him went down and fought against the Philistines; and David grew faint. 16 Then Ishbi-Benob, who was one of the sons of the giant, the weight of whose bronze spear was three hundred shekels, who was bearing a new sword, thought he could kill David. 17 But Abishai the son of Zeruiah came to his aid, and struck the Philistine and killed him. Then the men of David swore to him, saying, "You shall go out no more with us to battle, lest you quench the lamp of Israel."

18 Now it happened afterward that there was again a battle with the Philistines at Gob. Then Sibbechai the Hushathite killed Saph, who was one of the sons of the giant. 19 Again there was war at Gob with the Philistines, where Elhanan the son of Jaare-Oregim the Bethlehemite killed the brother of Goliath the Gittite, the shaft of whose spear was like a weaver's beam.

20 Yet again there was war at Gath, where there was a man of great stature, who had six fingers on each hand and six toes on each foot, twenty-four in number; and he also was born to the giant. 21 So when he defied Israel, Jonathan the son of Shimea, David's brother, killed him.

22 These four were born to the giant in Gath, and fell by the hand of David and by the hand of his servants.

EXPLORATION

1. The events in this passage likely occurred near the end of David's reign. How did Abishai demonstrate his courage and loyalty to David in the battle against Ishbi-Benob?

2. Why did David's men insist that he no longer go into battle after this encounter?

3. In particular, how did Sibbekai and Elhanan contribute to Israel's victories against the Philistines?

4. What was unique about the unnamed giant from the city of Gath?

5. Read 1 Samuel 17:25–26. What similarities do you see between Goliath's actions toward the Israelites and that of the giant from Gath?

6. How do these battles against the descendants of Rapha—each of whom were giants like Goliath—highlight the teamwork, bravery, and persistence of David and his men?

INSPIRATION

He vies for the bedside position, hoping to be the first voice you hear. He covets your waking thoughts. He awakes you with words of worry, stirs you with thoughts of stress. If you dread the day before you begin your day, mark it down: Your giant has been by your bed.

And he's just getting warmed up. He breathes down your neck as you eat your breakfast, whispers in your ear as you walk out the door, shadows your steps, and sticks to your hip. He checks your calendar, reads your mail, and talks trash to you.

"You ain't got what it takes."

"You come from a long line of losers."

"Fold your cards and leave the table. You've been dealt a bad hand."

He's your giant, your Goliath. Given half a chance, he'll turn your day into his Valley of Elah, taunting, teasing, boasting, and echoing claims from one hillside to the other.

Ever wonder why David took five stones into battle? Perhaps it's because he knew that one rock wouldn't do. Goliath had four behemoth relatives. "Ishbi-benob was a descendant of the giants; his bronze spearhead weighed more than seven pounds" (2 Samuel 21:16 NLT). Saph made the list, described as "another descendant of the giants" (verse 18 NLT).

Then there was "the brother of Goliath of Gath. The handle of his spear was as thick as a weaver's beam!" (verse 19 NLT). But these three seem harmless compared to King Kong: "There was a giant there [Gath] with six fingers on his hands and six toes on his feet—twenty-four fingers and toes! He was another of those descended from Rapha" (verse 20 MSG).

Why did David quarry a quintet of stones? Could it be because Goliath had four relatives the size of Tyrannosaurus rex? For all David knew, they would come running over the hill to defend their kin. David was ready to empty the chamber if that's what it took.

Goliaths still roam our world. Debt. Disaster. Dialysis. Danger. Deceit. Disease. Depression. Super-size challenges still swagger and strut, still pilfer sleep and embezzle peace and liposuction joy. But they can't dominate you. You know how to deal with them. You face giants by facing God first.

Focus on giants—you stumble.

Focus on God—your giants tumble.

You know what David knew, and so you do what David did. You pick up five stones and take them into battle. One prayer might not be enough. One apology might not do it. One day or month of resolve might not suffice. You may get knocked down a time or two . . . but don't quit. Keep loading the rocks. Keep swinging the sling.

David took five stones. You do the same. And the next time your Goliath wakes you up, reach for one. Odds are, he will be out of the room before you can even load your sling. (From *Facing Your Giants* by Max Lucado.)

REACTION

7. What "giants" are stealing your peace, hope, and confidence?

8. How are these giants showing up in your daily thoughts?

9. David picked up five stones to prepare for battle. What preparations do you need to make for the next time one of these giants attacks?

10. Read Luke 11:9–10. What does Jesus say about persisting in your prayers? What is given to the one who asks, seeks, and knocks?

11. Read James 1:2–3 and Romans 5:3–4. What do James and Paul say is being produced within you as you battle against your giants?

12. What would it look like to focus on the size of your God rather than the size of your foe the next time you encounter those giants?

LIFE LESSONS

Ishbi-Benob. Saph. Goliath's brother. An unnamed behemoth with extra fingers and toes. "These four were descendants of Rapha in Gath, and they fell at the hands of David and his men" (2 Samuel 21:22). What are we to make of this story? Clearly, one takeaway is that the Israelites had to persist in defeating the Philistine giants. But it's also interesting to note *how* this was done. David defeated Goliath on his own, but Abishai had to come to his aid to defeat Ishbi-Benob. Saph was killed by Sibbekai. Goliath's brother was defeated by Elhanan. Jonathan, a nephew of David, killed the unnamed giant. These descendants of Rapha were taken down by a *community* of warriors. In the same way, we have a community around us who can help us take down our giants. "Let us consider how we may spur one another on toward love and good deeds, not giving up meeting together, as some are in the habit of doing" (Hebrews 10:24–25).

DEVOTION

Lord God, thank you again for bringing me into your family and giving me fellow brothers and sisters in Christ. Help me to not be a lone warrior in my spiritual battles but to lean into the team of people you have provided to help me in the fight. Together, we will have the victory.

JOURNALING

How is God calling you to be persistent in prayer right now? Pick up your "five stones" and write out in detail what you want God to accomplish in that area of your life.

FOR FURTHER READING

To complete the book of 2 Samuel during this twelve-part study, read 2 Samuel 21:1–22:51. For more Bible passages about perseverance, read 1 Chronicles 16:11; Proverbs 24:15–16; Psalm 27:14; Matthew 24:12–13; Galatians 6:9; Timothy 2:12; James 1:12; Hebrews 12:1.

LESSON TWELVE

LOOKING BACK ON LIFE

"If my house were not right with God, surely he would not have made with me an everlasting covenant."
2 Samuel 23:5

REFLECTION

What is one act of God's goodness you can see clearly when you look back on your life?

SITUATION

The second "epilogue" story, told in 2 Samuel 21:15–22, related how David and his men killed four descendants of Rapha: Ishbi-Benob, Saph (or Sippai), Lahmi (who was Goliath's brother), and an unnamed giant with six fingers on each hand and six toes on each foot (see also 1 Chronicles 20:4–8). The next chapter, 2 Samuel 22, is comprised of a song that David offered to the Lord when he was delivered from the hand of Saul. David reflected on how God had equipped him with strength, trained his hands for battle, and made his enemies fall before him. He acknowledged the Lord's unwavering kindness and exalted him as the ultimate source of salvation. The beginning of the next chapter, 2 Samuel 23:1–7, contains David's final words.

OBSERVATION

Read 2 Samuel 23:1–7 and 1 Chronicles 28:2–10 from the New International Version or the New King James Version.

New International Version

23:1 These are the last words of David:

"The inspired utterance of David son of Jesse,
    the utterance of the man exalted by the Most High,
the man anointed by the God of Jacob,
    the hero of Israel's songs:

2 "The Spirit of the Lord spoke through me;
    his word was on my tongue.
3 The God of Israel spoke,
    the Rock of Israel said to me:
'When one rules over people in righteousness,

when he rules in the fear of God,
[4] he is like the light of morning at sunrise
on a cloudless morning,
like the brightness after rain
that brings grass from the earth.'

[5] "If my house were not right with God,
surely he would not have made with me an
everlasting covenant,
arranged and secured in every part;
surely he would not bring to fruition my salvation
and grant me my every desire."
[6] But evil men are all to be cast aside like thorns,
which are not gathered with the hand.
[7] Whoever touches thorns
uses a tool of iron or the shaft of a spear;
they are burned up where they lie."

[28:2] King David rose to his feet and said: "Listen to me, my fellow Israelites,
my people. I had it in my heart to build a house as a place of rest for the
ark of the covenant of the LORD, for the footstool of our God, and I made
plans to build it. [3] But God said to me, 'You are not to build a house for
my Name, because you are a warrior and have shed blood.'

[4] "Yet the LORD, the God of Israel, chose me from my whole family
to be king over Israel forever. He chose Judah as leader, and from the
tribe of Judah he chose my family, and from my father's sons he was
pleased to make me king over all Israel. [5] Of all my sons—and the LORD
has given me many—he has chosen my son Solomon to sit on the throne
of the kingdom of the LORD over Israel. [6] He said to me: 'Solomon your
son is the one who will build my house and my courts, for I have chosen
him to be my son, and I will be his father. [7] I will establish his kingdom
forever if he is unswerving in carrying out my commands and laws, as
is being done at this time.'

[8] "So now I charge you in the sight of all Israel and of the assembly of the LORD, and in the hearing of our God: Be careful to follow all the commands of the LORD your God, that you may possess this good land and pass it on as an inheritance to your descendants forever.

[9] "And you, my son Solomon, acknowledge the God of your father, and serve him with wholehearted devotion and with a willing mind, for the LORD searches every heart and understands every desire and every thought. If you seek him, he will be found by you; but if you forsake him,
he will reject you forever. [10] Consider now, for the LORD has chosen you
to build a house as the sanctuary. Be strong and do the work."

NEW KING JAMES VERSION

[23:1] Now these are the last words of David.

Thus says David the son of Jesse;
Thus says the man raised up on high,
The anointed of the God of Jacob,
And the sweet psalmist of Israel:

[2] "The Spirit of the LORD spoke by me,
And His word was on my tongue.
[3] The God of Israel said,
The Rock of Israel spoke to me:
'He who rules over men must be just,
Ruling in the fear of God.
[4] And he shall be like the light of the morning when the sun rises,
A morning without clouds,
Like the tender grass springing out of the earth,
By clear shining after rain.'

[5] "Although my house is not so with God,
Yet He has made with me an everlasting covenant,
Ordered in all things and secure.

For this is all my salvation and all my desire;
Will He not make it increase?
[6] But the sons of rebellion shall all be as thorns thrust away,
because they cannot be taken with hands.
[7] But the man who touches them
must be armed with iron and the shaft of a spear,
and they shall be utterly burned with fire in their place."

[28:2] Then King David rose to his feet and said, "Hear me, my brethren and
my people: I had it in my heart to build a house of rest for the ark of the
covenant of the LORD, and for the footstool of our God, and had made
preparations to build it. [3] But God said to me, 'You shall not build a house
for My name, because you have been a man of war and have shed blood.'
[4] However the LORD God of Israel chose me above all the house of
my father to be king over Israel forever, for He has chosen Judah to be the
ruler. And of the house of Judah, the house of my father, and among the
sons of my father, He was pleased with me to make me king over all Israel.
[5] And of all my sons (for the LORD has given me many sons) He has chosen my son Solomon to sit on the throne of the kingdom of the LORD over
Israel. [6] Now He said to me, 'It is your son Solomon who shall build My
house and My courts; for I have chosen him to be My son, and I will be his
Father. [7] Moreover I will establish his kingdom forever, if he is steadfast to
observe My commandments and My judgments, as it is this day.'
[8] Now therefore, in the sight of all Israel, the assembly of the LORD,
and in the hearing of our God, be careful to seek out all the commandments of the LORD your God, that you may possess this good land, and
leave it as an inheritance for your children after you forever.
[9] "As for you, my son Solomon, know the God of your father, and
serve Him with a loyal heart and with a willing mind; for the LORD
searches all hearts and understands all the intent of the thoughts. If you
seek Him, He will be found by you; but if you forsake Him, He will cast
you off forever. [10] Consider now, for the LORD has chosen you to build a
house for the sanctuary; be strong, and do it."

EXPLORATION

1. How does David describe himself in 2 Samuel 23:1? What does he say in verses 2–4 about the kind of ruler God had called him to be?

2. What does David say about his "house" in verse 5? What is his conclusion in verses 6–7 about those who choose to be enemies of God?

3. According to 1 Chronicles 28:2–3, what was one of David's unfulfilled plans? Why did God instead choose Solomon to accomplish this task?

4. What conditions did God give in verses 6–7 for Solomon's kingdom to be established forever? What was required on Solomon's part for this promise to be met?

5. What advice did David give to Solomon in verses 8–10 as the younger man prepared to assume the throne of Israel?

6. How does David's overall charge in these passages to Solomon and the people of Israel emphasize the importance of following God's commands and seeking his will?

INSPIRATION

A temple. David had wanted to build a temple. What he had done for Israel, he wanted to do for the ark—protect it. What he had done with Jerusalem, he wanted to do with the temple—establish it. And who better than he to do so? Hadn't he, literally, written the book on worship? Didn't he rescue the ark of the covenant? The temple would have been his swan song, his signature deed. David had expected to dedicate his final years to building a shrine to God.

At least, that had been his intention. "I had intended to build a permanent home for the ark of the covenant of the LORD and for the footstool of our God. So I had made preparations to build it" (1 Chronicles 28:2 NASB). *Preparations.* Architects chosen. Builders selected. Blueprints and plans, drawings and numbers. Temple columns sketched. Steps designed.

"I had intended . . . I had made preparations . . ."

Intentions. Preparations. But no temple. Why? Did David grow discouraged? No. He stood willing. Were the people resistant? Hardly. They gave generously. Were the resources scarce? Far from it. David "supplied more bronze than could be weighed, and . . . more cedar logs than could be counted" (22:3–4 NCV). Then what happened?

A conjunction happened.

Conjunctions operate as the signal lights of sentences. Some, such as *and*, are green. Others, such as *however*, are yellow. A few are red. Sledgehammer red. They stop you.

David got a red light. "I had made preparations to build it. *But* God said to me, 'You shall not build a house for My name, because you are a man of war and have shed blood" (28:2–3 NASB, emphasis added). David's bloodthirsty temperament cost him the temple privilege.

What do you do with the "but God" moments in life? When God interrupts your good plans, how do you respond? David followed the "but God" with a "yet God." He said, "Yet the LORD, the God of Israel, chose me from my whole family to be king over Israel forever . . . from my father's sons he was pleased to make me king over all Israel" (28:4).

Reduce the paragraph to a phrase and it reads, "Who am I to complain?" Looking back, there was so much he could say about his life. He had been "exalted by the Most High," "anointed by the God of Jacob," and was "the hero of Israel's songs" (2 Samuel 23:1). He was the one with whom God had chosen to make "an everlasting covenant" (verse 5).

David had gone from runt to royalty, from herding sheep to leading armies, from sleeping in the pasture to living in the palace. When you are given an ice cream sundae, you don't complain over a missing cherry. (From *Facing Your Giants* by Max Lucado.)

REACTION

7. When is a time that God interrupted or redirected one of your plans? How did you know it was God who was closing that particular door?

8. How did you respond when God interrupted or redirected your plan in that way?

9. When has God called on you to support another person in the way that he called on David to support Solomon? How willing were you to accept that role?

10. David followed his "but God" statement with a "yet God" affirmation. What did David recognize about the Lord in that moment?

11. What are some of the "yet God" affirmations you can make? What are some of God's acts toward you for which you are especially grateful?

12. What is God calling you to remember today about his good intentions toward you?

LIFE LESSONS

The final chapters in 2 Samuel highlight the loyalty and bravery of David's men, whom God used to bring about great victories (see 23:8–39), and the consequences of David's prideful act in ordering a census of Israel, after which he repents and intercedes for his people (see 24:1–25). In many ways, these chapters sum up the contrasts in David's life: great spiritual victories, resulting in blessings from the Lord, but also great spiritual failures, resulting in consequences from the Lord. David was "a man after [God's] own heart" (1 Samuel 13:14), but that doesn't mean he always had the Lord's interests at heart. David's life was a portrait of success and failure, but what set him apart was his deep desire to follow God's will—and his willingness to repent when he stumbled. In this regard, David truly serves as a role model for us all.

DEVOTION

Heavenly Father, when my time on this earth is coming to an end, I want to be able to look back on my life without regrets. Help me to be a person whom others will remember as being kind, forgiving, generous, joyful, and loving. I want them to see you when they look at my life.

JOURNALING

What legacy do you want to leave? Write out at least five things you want people to remember about you when your time on earth has ended.

FOR FURTHER READING

To complete the book of 2 Samuel during this twelve-part study, read 2 Samuel 23:1–24:25. For more Bible passages about God's goodness, read 1 Chronicles 16:34; Psalm 34:8; Lamentations 3:22–23; Nahum 1:7; Matthew 7:11; Romans 8:28; 2 Timothy 2:13; James 1:17.

LEADER'S GUIDE FOR SMALL GROUPS

Thank you for your willingness to lead a group through *Life Lessons from 2 Samuel.* The rewards of being a leader are different from those of participating, and we hope you find your own walk with Jesus deepened by this experience. During the twelve lessons in this study, you will guide your group through selected passages in 2 Samuel and explore the key themes of the book. There are several elements in this leader's guide that will help you as you structure your study and reflection time, so be sure to follow along and take advantage of each one.

BEFORE YOU BEGIN

Before your first meeting, make sure the group members have their own copy of the *Life Lessons from 2 Samuel* study guide so they can follow along and have their answers written out ahead of time. Alternately, you can hand out the guides at your first meeting and give the group some time to look over the material and ask any preliminary questions. Be sure to send a sheet around the room during that first meeting and have the members write down their name, phone number, and email address so you can keep in touch with them during the week.

There are several ways to structure the duration of the study. You can cover each lesson individually for a total of twelve weeks, or you can combine two lessons together per week for a total of six weeks of discussion.

You can also choose to have the group members read just the selected passages of Scripture given in each lesson, or they can cover the entire book of 2 Samuel by reading the material listed in the "For Further Reading" section at the end of each lesson. The following table illustrates these options:

Twelve-Week Format

Week	Lessons Covered	Simplified Reading	Expanded Reading
1	The Loss of a Friend	2 Samuel 1:1–16	2 Samuel 1:1–27
2	Following God's Guidance	2 Samuel 2:1–17	2 Samuel 2:1–3:39
3	Overcoming Strongholds	2 Samuel 5:1–25	2 Samuel 4:1–5:25
4	God Comes on His Terms	2 Samuel 6:1–19	2 Samuel 6:1–23
5	An Eternal Covenant	2 Samuel 7:1–17	2 Samuel 7:1–8:18
6	A Promise to Keep	2 Samuel 9:1–13	2 Samuel 9:1–10:19
7	Colossal Collapses	2 Samuel 11:1–17	2 Samuel 11:1–27
8	A Sentence Levied	2 Samuel 12:1–14	2 Samuel 12:1–14:33
9	Family Betrayals	2 Samuel 15:1–18	2 Samuel 15:1–17:29
10	The Return of the King	2 Samuel 19:9–23	2 Samuel 18:1–20:26
11	Taking Down Giants	2 Samuel 21:15–22	2 Samuel 21:1–22:51
12	Looking Back on Life	2 Samuel 23:1–7; 1 Chronicles 28:2–10	2 Samuel 23:1–24:25

Six-Week Format

Week	Lessons Covered	Simplified Reading	Expanded Reading
1	The Loss of a Friend / Following God's Guidance	2 Samuel 1:1–16; 2:1–17	2 Samuel 1:1–3:39
2	Overcoming Strongholds / God Comes on His Terms	2 Samuel 5:1–6:19	2 Samuel 4:1–6:23
3	An Eternal Covenant / A Promise to Keep	2 Samuel 7:1–17; 9:1–13	2 Samuel 7:1–10:19

Week	Lessons Covered	Simplified Reading	Expanded Reading
4	Colossal Collapses / A Sentence Levied	2 Samuel 11:1–17; 12:1–14	2 Samuel 11:1–14:33
5	Family Betrayals / The Return of the King	2 Samuel 15:1–18; 19:9–23	2 Samuel 15:1–20:26
6	Taking Down Giants / Looking Back on Life	2 Samuel 21:15–22; 23:1–7; 1 Chronicles 28:2–10	2 Samuel 21:1–24:25

Generally, the ideal size you will want for the group is between eight to ten people, which ensures everyone will have enough time to participate in discussions. If you have more people, you might want to break up the main group into smaller subgroups. Encourage those who show up at the first meeting to commit to attending the duration of the study, as this will help the group members get to know each other, create stability for the group, and help you know how to prepare each week.

Each of the lessons begins with a brief reflection that highlights the theme you will be discussing that week. As you begin your group time, have the group members briefly respond to the opening question to get them thinking about the topic at hand. Some people may want to tell a long story in response to one of these questions, but the goal is to keep the answers brief. Ideally, you want everyone in the group to get a chance to answer, so try to keep the responses to just a few minutes. If you have more talkative group members, say up front that everyone needs to limit his or her answer to two minutes.

Give the group members a chance to answer, but tell them to feel free to pass if they wish. With the rest of the study, it's generally not a good idea to have everyone answer every question—a free-flowing discussion is more desirable. But with the opening reflection question, you can go around the circle. Encourage shy people to share, but don't force them.

Before your first meeting, let the group members know how the lessons are broken down. During your group discussion time the members will be drawing on the answers they wrote for the Exploration and Reaction sections, so encourage them to always complete these ahead of time. Also, invite them to bring any questions and insights they uncovered to your next meeting, especially if they had a breakthrough moment or if they didn't understand something they read.

WEEKLY PREPARATION

As the leader, there are a few things that you should do to prepare for each meeting:

- *Read through the lesson.* This will help you to become familiar with the content and know how to structure the discussion times.
- *Decide which questions you want to discuss.* Depending on how you structure your group time, you may not be able to cover every question. So select the questions ahead of time that you absolutely want the group to explore.
- *Be familiar with the questions you want to discuss.* When the group meets you'll be watching the clock, so you want to make sure you are familiar with the Bible study questions you have selected. You can then spend time in the passage again when the group meets. In this way, you'll ensure you have the passage more deeply in your mind than your group members.
- *Pray for your group.* Pray for your group members throughout the week and ask God to lead them as they study his Word.
- *Bring extra supplies to your meeting.* The members should bring their own pens for writing notes, but it's a good idea to have extras available for those who forget. You may also want to bring paper and additional Bibles.

Note that in many cases there will not be one "right" answer to the question. Answers will vary, especially when the group members are being asked to share their personal experiences.

STRUCTURING THE DISCUSSION TIME

You will need to determine with your group how long you want to meet each week so you can plan your time accordingly. Generally, most groups like to meet for either sixty minutes or ninety minutes, so you could use one of the following schedules:

Section	60 Minutes	90 Minutes
WELCOME (members arrive and get settled)	5 minutes	10 minutes
REFLECTION (discuss the opening question for the lesson)	10 minutes	15 minutes
DISCUSSION (discuss the Bible study questions in the Exploration and Reaction sections)	35 minutes	50 minutes
PRAYER/CLOSING (pray together as a group and dismiss)	10 minutes	15 minutes

As the group leader, it is up to you to keep track of the time and keep things moving along according to your schedule. You might want to set a timer for each segment so both you and the group members know when your time is up. (Note that there are some good phone apps for timers that play a gentle chime or other pleasant sound instead of a disruptive noise.) Don't feel pressured to cover every question you have selected if the group has a good discussion going. Again, it's not necessary to go around the circle and make everyone share.

Don't be concerned if the group members are silent or slow to share. People are often quiet when they are pulling together their ideas, and this might be a new experience for them. Just ask a question and let it hang in the air until someone shares. You can then say, "Thank you. What about others? What came to you when you reflected on the passage?"

GROUP DYNAMICS

Leading a group through *Life Lessons from 2 Samuel* will prove to be highly rewarding both to you and your group members—but that doesn't mean you will not encounter any challenges along the way! Discussions can get off track. Group members may not be sensitive to the needs and ideas of others. Some might worry they will be expected to talk about matters that make them feel awkward. Others may express comments that result in disagreements. To help ease this strain on you and the group, consider the following ground rules:

- When someone raises a question or comment that is off the main topic, suggest you deal with it another time, or, if you feel led to go in that direction, let the group know you will be spending some time discussing it.
- If someone asks a question you don't know how to answer, admit it and move on. At your discretion, invite group members to comment on questions that call for personal experience.
- If you find one or two people are dominating the discussion time, direct a few questions to others in the group. Outside the main group time, ask the more dominating members to help you draw out the quieter ones. Work to make them a part of the solution instead of the problem.
- When a disagreement occurs, encourage the group members to process the matter in love. Encourage those on opposite sides to restate what they heard the other side say about the matter, and then invite each side to evaluate if that perception is accurate. Lead the group in examining other Scriptures related to the topic and look for common ground.

When any of these issues arise, encourage your members to follow these words: "Love one another" (John 13:34), "If it is possible, as far as it depends on you, live at peace with everyone" (Romans 12:18), and, "Be quick to listen, slow to speak and slow to become angry" (James 1:19).

Thank you again for taking the time to lead your group. May God reward your efforts and dedication and make your time together in this study fruitful for his kingdom.

More Encouragement from Max Lucado

The Max Lucado Encouraging Word Podcast is all about the greatest story ever told—the living Savior who brings you a lifetime of hope.

Listen wherever you enjoy podcasts.

Max's YouTube show FRESH HOPE features timeless, encouraging teaching. Each episode will shift our focus from our worried, weary world to our good God and the refreshing promises found in his Word.

Watch and subscribe on YouTube.com/MaxLucadoOfficial

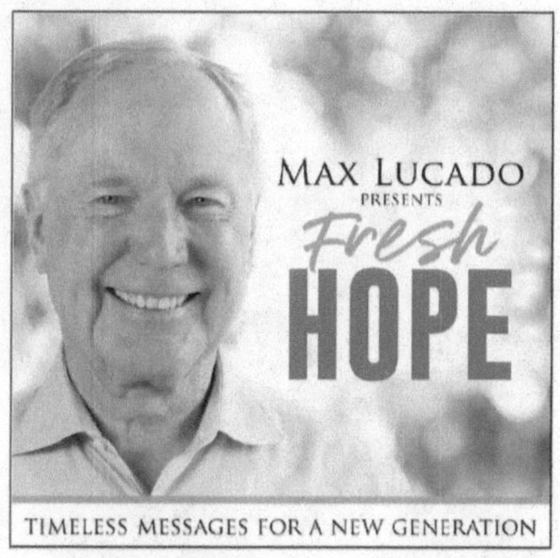

BIBLE STUDIES INCLUDE

Genesis
Psalms
Ezra & Nehemiah
Daniel & Esther
Matthew
Mark
Luke
John
Acts
Romans
1 Corinthians
2 Corinthians
Galatians
Ephesians
Philippians
Colossians & Philemon
1 & 2 Thessalonians
1 & 2 Timothy & Titus
Hebrews
James
1 & 2 Peter
1, 2, 3 John & Jude
Revelation

HARPERCHRISTIANRESOURCES.COM

From the Publisher

GREAT STUDIES

ARE EVEN BETTER WHEN THEY'RE SHARED!

Help others find this study

- Post a review at your favorite online bookseller
- Post a picture on a social media account and share why you enjoyed it
- Send a note to a friend who would also love it—or better yet, go through it with them!

Thanks for helping others grow their faith!

www.ingramcontent.com/pod-product-compliance
Lightning Source LLC
LaVergne TN
LVHW030921080826
845145LV00013B/2999

9780310170976